A Punkhouse in the Deep South

UNIVERSITY PRESS OF FLORIDA

Florida A&M University, Tallahassee
Florida Atlantic University, Boca Raton
Florida Gulf Coast University, Ft. Myers
Florida International University, Miami
Florida State University, Tallahassee
New College of Florida, Sarasota
University of Central Florida, Orlando
University of Florida, Gainesville
University of North Florida, Jacksonville
University of South Florida, Tampa
University of West Florida, Pensacola

# A PUNKHOUSE

University Press of Florida

Gainesville · Tallahassee · Tampa · Boca Raton

Pensacola · Orlando · Miami · Jacksonville · Ft. Myers · Sarasota

# IN THE DEEP SOUTH

## The Oral History of 309

Aaron Cometbus and Scott Satterwhite

26  25  24  23  22  21   6  5  4  3  2  1

ISBN 978-0-8130-6852-7
Library of Congress Control Number: 2021930641

The University Press of Florida is the scholarly publishing agency for the State University
System of Florida, comprising Florida A&M University, Florida Atlantic University, Florida
Gulf Coast University, Florida International University, Florida State University, New College
of Florida, University of Central Florida, University of Florida, University of North Florida,
University of South Florida, and University of West Florida.

University Press of Florida
2046 NE Waldo Road
Suite 2100
Gainesville, FL 32609
http://upress.ufl.edu

# CONTENTS

A Punkhouse in the Deep South

# Introduction

Rather than telling the story of 309 using select quotes and an impartial voice, we decided to let the residents speak for themselves, each narrating the punkhouse's twenty-five year history in turn. Just a few explanations are required before we begin, starting with the title and its terms.

When punk gets defined, it's usually as a style of music that's amateurish, obnoxious, and raw. The word has come to describe anything—fashion, food, politicians—with a cutting edge. For its adherents, however, raising one's voice or learning three chords is only the start. Personal transformation is just half of the do-it-yourself process, hand-in-hand with offering your support.

In short, punk is a pyramid scheme, the payoff being membership in an exclusive club that shares resources and provides encouragement. To buy in, all you need to do is take part—and to have faith, which is sometimes hard. Uncritical support means you can pick a self-destructive path, or form a horrible band, and there'll still be a crowd to cheer you on.

One would expect a movement based on participation to be studied from the perspective of its participants. Instead, most books on punk focus on individuals or bands that rose *above* the crowd. Only a handful of scholarly texts look into the ethics and belief systems on which punk is based. As for punk's great unwashed and how they actually live, there is hardly a trace.

That's where punkhouses come in. As the name implies, these are houses where punks live. The manners in which these spaces function—or are dysfunctional—reflect punk's values and priorities. The model is rooted in communal living experiments in the seventies and the squatting movement in the eighties. The anarchist Dial House near London, home of the band Crass, is a close antecedent.

Still, a punkhouse is decidedly different. A punkhouse is not a commune. A punkhouse is not a crash pad.

Very well, then what *is* a punkhouse? What makes a living space inviting to punks and intimidating to everyone else? And how can a communal residence get passed down through multiple generations and still maintain its character without any written charter or rules?

These are not questions we asked, but ones answered by the 309 residents nonetheless.

To set the scene, we invite the reader to picture a windswept, low-lying city at the westernmost edge of the Florida panhandle. The population is fairly small in number, making the ten or more miscreants living in a large, dilapidated house on the wrong side of the tracks stand out in relief.

## My Florida

Because of punk's emphasis on individuality and distrust of centralized authority, its music and literature often have a regional flavor and a distinctive sense of place. As a result, we can sing along with two Pensacola punk bands to evoke the landscape, starting with the legendary and somewhat comical eighties combo Maggot Sandwich:

> *Two hundred city blocks of shotgun shacks along the street*
> *The kids look hungry, the old they suffer from the heat*
> *Old abandoned cars are the toys with which they play*
> *The world that made them mean just gets tougher every day*
> *This ain't no hot nightspot*
> *This ain't no fancy suit*
> *This ain't no fast sports car*
> *This is the Sunshine State, my Florida!*

As singer Vic Kaos points out, Pensacola lacks the usual Florida archetypes. Rather than a tourist trap or state college, its main draw is a Navy base. There's no Disney World or Everglades, few Cuban exiles or elderly Jews. Culturally, economically, and geographically it belongs more to the Deep South. Alabama is a stone's throw away, Miami a twelve-hour drive.

Another local band, This Bike is a Pipe Bomb—who formed and lived at 309—bring it closer to home with their "Board of Tourism":

*We kill abortion doctors*
*We got albino squirrels*
*We got the whitest beaches . . .*
*We got a drive-thru funeral home*
*You know they even filmed a movie there once*
*It had James Brown in it*
*And they gave away hotdogs*

"Ted Bundy was caught behind the Hot Cake King," is the song's rousing refrain, and Pensacola's main claim to fame.

## What Came First, the Band or the City?

Perhaps you've wondered where Band of Five Flags got their name. The flags reflect different eras of influence in Pensacola's long history—eras of punk in the case of the band, who covered songs by local groups, like Bulletproof and Headless Marines.

The city had the tagline first, it must be admitted. The flags of Spain, France, and England have long flown downtown alongside the familiar stars and stripes, as if the city were split into quarters of occupation, like postwar Berlin. Until recently, the Confederate flag completed the count. Activist pressure forced it to be replaced by the Florida flag, on which the state seal appears to be crossed out.

Pensacola's other title, "first city," is more dubious, though the signage can be seen on everything from art centers to beauty supply shops. Spanish conquistador Don Tristan de Luna landed in present-day Pensacola in 1559, but a massive hurricane immediately struck, and most of his ships—including the expedition's supplies—were sunk. If he'd been successful, Pensacola would be the oldest continuously inhabited city in the United States. Instead, the title actually belongs to St. Augustine.

Pensacola can't even boast having the country's oldest continually inhabited punkhouse; that honor goes to either Carbondale, Oakland, or Washington, DC. Yet for a city humbled by having its ass kicked regularly by hurricanes, fourth place is still pretty good—and a familiar role, since Atlanta, New Orleans, and Tallahassee are all roughly two hundred miles away, bigger if not older siblings that traditionally leave Pensacola in the shade.

When Andrew Jackson ordered the invasion of Spanish Florida, part of his impetus was crushing an armed slave rebellion just outside of Pensacola. Jackson, a slave owner, was concerned about the maroon colonies in Florida rising up, and he forced Spain to surrender the state. Even after Florida seceded in the Civil War, parts of the Pensacola region remained in Union hands, and the city's entire Confederate history lasted less than two years. Despite the brutal backlash against African Americans following Reconstruction—including lynchings in Plaza Ferdinand, the city's town square—a culture of resistance arose. A chapter of Marcus Garvey's Universal Negro Improvement Association formed, the NAACP recruited, and segregation was legally challenged in the courts. Boycotts, strikes, protests, and sit-ins became part of the landscape as early as 1905.

Culturally, Pensacola was a crossroad in the early days of jazz and blues, with composer Don Shirley learning to play piano in St. Cyprian's Church, and Ma Rainey gracing stages downtown. To commemorate this history, Pensacola has one of the few Blues Trail markers outside of Mississippi. Country music legend Hank Williams, though not a native, became familiar with the city in the manner many visitors do—by accompanying his aged father on trips to the V.A. hospital. No congressional district in the country contains as many military veterans as Pensacola's.

The city continues to grow and change, in tiny increments rather than leaps and bounds, but it's noteworthy that the tourists who once turned Pensacola into the "Redneck Riviera" every Memorial Day weekend turn it into the "Gay Riviera" now.

**Big House by the Tracks**

When punks first moved into 309 6th Avenue, the area was racially and economically mixed. Massive Victorian-style homes sat next to utilitarian shotgun shacks. Longtime homeowners lived near short-term renters. The House of God, lit with its bright red neon sign, filled the streets with gospel music during Sunday services. Cars lined up at the drive-through window at Junior's Funeral Home, though it was later shuttered after flashers were caught exposing themselves to the stiffs.

Adjacent to downtown, Old East Hill felt like its own small village—casual, compact, and easy to traverse on foot or bike—markedly different from the rest of Pensacola with its strip malls and sprawl. The railroad depot was gone, but freight trains still passed through the neighborhood day and night, equally comforting and unnerving, carrying coal and orange juice during peacetime and tanks during times of war. End of the Line Cafe, one of several businesses that began at 309, derived its name from the rails that bring the street to a dead-end.

One might see a few illegal passengers jump off a train as it slowed down to take the curve in front of the local gay bar. More often than not, the travelers hoisted their packs and proceeded to the front porch of 309, having heard about the house through their own underground networks.

Sometimes, baking in the Florida rotisserie, a punk sat outside waiting to greet them.


## Whose Fault Is This?

In 2016, a campaign was launched by former residents to purchase the house and turn it into a punk museum. Curating "Punksacola: Reflections of a Subculture," an exhibit at the T.T. Wentworth, Jr. Museum, was their first step to publicize the cause and gather a permanent collection.

Dr. Jamin Wells, a professor at the University of West Florida, saw the exhibit and decided 309 would be an interesting subject for his undergraduate oral history class. In February and March of 2020, Wells dispatched a dozen students to seek out current and former residents of 309, record their stories, and find out how living in the punkhouse affected their lives.

The original plan was simply to create two comb-bound keepsakes from Well's 309 Oral History Project: one for the UWF Historic Trust and the other for the newly formed 309 Punk Museum. Yet when the participants looked over their transcripts, they found an unexpected surprise. Each person told the story of the house, but only knew their own part. When combined, the narratives unfolded like a game of Exquisite Corpse, hilarious and only sometimes matching up.

The students added to the entertainment by tripping over topics unfamiliar and outside their comfort zones. Their distance from—and occasional disgust with—the subjects discussed proved to be a huge boon, for it forced the participants to explain their beliefs in detail, without shared references or shorthand phrases. In fact, talking to strangers made it easier for them to open up.

For the present and former 309 residents, reading the transcripts was like meeting each other again for the first time. There was so much personal history we had missed or never thought to ask. There were feelings we hadn't had the guts to admit, or didn't understand ourselves until decades had passed. Two of us decided to edit the interviews for clarity, ask a few follow-up questions, and shape the collective narrative into a volume for public release.

Doing so is not an attempt to tell the story of punk, or even its particular history in Pensacola. But we do tell *our* story of punk—one set in an unlikely city, in a house rich with history, and filled with day-to-day details of the culture, which have not been documented enough. The voices here help fill gaps in many narratives, including Southern cultural studies. Simply put, the South is not always as it appears, and its subcultures and countercultures are an intrinsic part of its makeup.

Most importantly, for the first time in nonfiction, this book examines in depth what living in a punkhouse is like. By looking at a single house and its evolving and revolving residents, it shows how people create community far outside of societal norms and challenge the standard definition of family.

Here, then, is a group of people making a conscious choice to live as morally, honestly, and freely as possible, and the many challenges and rewards they encounter along the way.

# Skott Cowgill

"I was coming out of the fire
and I needed a place to land"

**We'd like to get some background information, which is what we do with these oral history interviews. Where were you born?**

Cowgill: Rhode Island. But I spent most of my formative years in Pensacola.

**Tell me about your parents.**

Cowgill: Let's see, my dad was an FBI agent. My mom was really sick. My dad moved around a lot because of the job, and we landed in Pensacola because they had doctors that were available to do laser surgery—that was a new concept at the time—to correct my mom's vision, or to allow her to see. That's why we moved to Pensacola originally. I don't know, I got kicked out when I was seventeen.

**Do you have any special memories from your childhood?**

Cowgill: I wasn't really into it. I guess a special memory would be that my dad had a record collection, so I found a way to be locked in a room and listen on headphones to music. It was good for them because at least I was isolated and not causing any problems. I spent a lot of time just sitting in that room listening to albums over and over again. For some reason it brought me a lot of calm and was very interesting to me—the music world.

**Where'd you go to school?**

Cowgill: I went to Creative Learning Center, I went to Episcopal Day School. In New Orleans, I went to Jefferson Academy. But I was always a troublemaker, super hyperactive, always causing problems, so I went to a lot of schools. I went to Catholic school and got kicked out of there. I went to Woodham but only lasted a couple of days there, and I got kicked out of Pensacola High School because I wrote "suicidal" down my leg. I was into this band called Suicidal Tendencies and I didn't realize that was a problem. Then I went to Washington High School. I got kicked out of that. I eventually graduated from [Pensacola Private School of] Liberal Arts because I think they probably would take anybody. It was a good school, though, and they were doing some interesting stuff.

**Okay, tell me about your earliest memories of the 309 punkhouse.**

Cowgill: I was coming out of the fire and I needed a place to land. Terry Johnson had been very helpful in the whole situation. She was the owner at Sluggo's, and we were really good friends. She found this place, and there was a big room available. The guys that lived there— one of the guys was on house arrest, the other was drinking himself into a stupor. There wasn't much going on there, and there wasn't much furniture either. But she secured the spot for me and got me the big room in the front, and it looked pretty great. So I moved in there, and those guys slowly started moving out. We started moving in all of our friends and people in the punk community, and it started gaining momentum.

**Can you tell me about the neighborhood around the house during that time?**

Cowgill: There wasn't much around. The tracks were right there, so trainhoppers would hop on, hop off, and sometimes they would come in, and we'd put them up for the night. It was near the Civic Center. Van Gogh's was there, which was a coffee place—it was a little overpriced, but it had a porch area in the back. It was really kind of a nice neighborhood, actually.

**Can you describe what the house looked like then, how it was arranged?**

Cowgill: We had a ramp in the back that the people before us had built. It had gotten rotten, but we had re-plied it and fixed it up. It was a two-story building, and there was a large porch on the front where we spent many hours eating boiled peanuts and discussing politics, and how to take over. There was a little side yard where we planted watermelons and various fruits and vegetables. Most of them didn't work, but occasionally some came through. It was gray with white trim, and it overlooked a very quiet street. I think that's all I got.

**If I understand correctly, you lived at the house for a number of years?**

Cowgill: Yeah, I was the first one to move in and start moving our folks in there. Terry moved me in there, and then slowly our old acquaintances and comrades started moving in.

**Why did you decide to live there?**

Cowgill: Because I needed a spot, and with the size of the place the rent was very agreeable. And when we met the landlord, J.P., he was a really good guy. Kind of a mellow surfer guy but into philosophy, and he backed us quite a bit on the things we needed fixed. For a landlord to work with a bunch of crazy looking punks is rare, because most of the time that's something you hide from the landlord. This guy we actually liked seeing, and when he'd show up we'd hang out with him.

So that was another reason to do it. Plus, we just needed a punkhouse. But the selling point was the ramp in the back. Having a ramp was a huge thing for us, huge thing for me. All the sessions we had back there, and all the people that skated there—there were some really great skaters that came through. So that was definitely a big selling point.

**Can you walk me through a typical day at the punkhouse?**

Cowgill: Because I worked at Sluggo's late at night, I'd wake up about 1:00 kind of groggy, get some coffee. Maybe go down to the Yellow Store—they called it that because it was painted yellow—and get some boiled peanuts, Hawk's Boiled Peanuts. Uh, sit on the porch and eat the boiled peanuts, throw the shells in the front there, and then I'd start painting. I'd go in my room and turn the stereo on full blast. I'd just paint, and then about an hour into painting somebody would knock on the door, and it would either be a Food Not Bombs[1] thing or a protest that we had to do.

I would try to finish my painting, but I had to go to the protest. So we would go to the protest, it would last about two hours. We usually outnumbered the other people there. At Food Not Bombs we outnumbered the people we were feeding. There's maybe ten people who were really stoked that we were there serving, but there were fifteen of us.

When we finished that up, we'd come home. We would have a group meal because some of the people that lived there were vegan chefs, like

---

1  An organization providing healthy, vegetarian food to the hungry through thousands of independent local chapters.

Rymodee and Shari, and they made incredible food. It would be a huge meal, and a lot of times there would be a show that night, so we'd get ready to see whatever band we were going to go see. After that it would be late night skate sessions. If it was summertime we'd go to the beach. That was always good because the beach was only fifteen minutes away.

**What are your fondest memories from that period?**

Cowgill: All of them [laughs]. All the people that were involved were really great. There was an anarchist school going on. If you didn't want to do that, you could learn to cook with all these people that later on became incredibly good chefs, like Jen Knight. When we started doing veganism nobody knew anything about it, so we were just eating salads and basically garbage. People got sick of that so they started learning how to cook. I didn't, but the rest of the crew really took off, and some of them made careers out of it.

There was the Spare Change Cafe, which was a vegan cafe that we were all running in 309. Sometimes the trainhoppers would come off the train, and they were amazed because we took it really seriously. I would be a waiter, a snooty waiter guy. I would sit everybody down, and they were nervous because of how much it would cost. But then you would tell all three of them, it's a dollar. Also, I had a bar in the front called the Speakeasy. It only opened on Mondays, but it was a good place for people to get together and work on their ideas, plan for things to come, or organize a protest.

So it was a good learning house, and everyone got along really well. The idea was that you were so bored in the town, so you would want to do something positive. You were always trying to book shows, or set up something, or start a bookstore, or do a zine. There were so many zines. You were writing and writing and writing, sending it out to other cities. You were constantly challenged for good things instead of just sitting around drinking beer. That happened too, but after you did all of the work.

**I understand. Are you a vegan?**

Cowgill: No, I'm not, but I was at the time, for a really long time. I'm more of a strict vegetarian.

**What kind of protests did you go to?**

Cowgill: Well, when the war was around we were protesting constantly—also when the Klan was around, we'd protest the Klan. Everybody would get together with signs and stuff and we had built our numbers up pretty big, so we usually outnumbered whatever the problem was.

**What were some challenges that you faced while living at the punkhouse?**

Cowgill: The thing is, it was an easy lifestyle because everyone got along really well and were about similar causes. Instead of having roommates that were not into what you were doing, everyone was pushing everybody to do more. Oftentimes you didn't have enough time to yourself because you were so busy. That was kind of a challenge, but a good challenge because it motivated people.

**Why did you eventually leave the house?**

Cowgill: I had been painting—painting was my main thing at the time—but I had exhausted all the galleries in Pensacola, and most of the ones in New Orleans I could get into, and there was no place else to show. So I was interested in moving to San Francisco, where you throw a rock, you hit an artist. I thought it would be a better environment for my art, selling art, which turned out to be true. You do lose the community that you had, unfortunately. San Francisco is definitely more isolated, but there's more opportunity.

**I'm going to ask you a bit of a broad question. What does punk mean to you?**

Cowgill: The base of it is to bring up the people around you. Making everyone more aware of things that are wrong about the world—like racism, sexism, and homophobia—and trying to combat them. To bring new people into it, and learn those idealisms, but also constantly work to make things better.

It's based, of course, on music as well, but if you listen to a lot of the lyrics, that's what they're about. They're about positivity, about strength in numbers, about a bunch of people who were misfits for one reason or another but were accepted in the punk community. Even if you didn't know much about punk, in Pensacola especially they were willing to teach you—to help you learn about these new bands and new concepts and ideas. It was like college for people who weren't going to college. A different kind of college. Human rights college.

**Can you tell me what your first introduction to the Pensacola punk scene was like?**

Cowgill: Oh, that's a tough one. I guess I was a skater first, and there were seven or eight of us in high school that skated. All the football players hated us and were always beating us up, but we sort of banded together to stop that from happening. I started picking up records that were skate-related. I went to a record store called the Sound Box, which had a punk section—it was a small crate that just said "punk" on it. There were maybe fifteen records in it. I went through the records, and anything with a skull on it I'd take out because I thought skulls were cool, because I was a kid. I started reading zines—*Maximum Rocknroll, Flipside*—and immersing myself in, and trying to understand, this whole culture of punk. I started writing my own zine, and constantly listening to records and, uh, playing air guitar in the mirror. I felt so alienated in society, in school or whatever. Then I realized other people had this same thought, and that brought us together as a tight-knit group.

**What was your zine?**

Cowgill: I did a zine called *Smell of Dead Fish.* I did like sixty-five issues total. I did that for years. It had a lot of ecology stuff, and it would evolve as my politics evolved. Originally there was a lot of skate photos—blurry photos, you can't even see what's going on. Then there would be freelance writing, record reviews, and as I got more involved, I spent more time with it. I think that was the first zine, and definitely the longest running zine, in Pensacola. But I also did a lot of side zines. I did *Sparrow,* which was written by all women. I did *Stranded in the Ice in Austin,* and *When Punk Turns 30.*

**How did your involvement with the punk scene change you over time?**

Cowgill: As I started putting on shows and learning how to do things more efficiently, it just got better. I learned a lot from the people around because they were working on stuff constantly as well—like Scott Satterwhite, for instance, and Aaron Cometbus. He was an influence in the zine world for me. I met Aaron when I booked Crimpshrine at the Mix, and we had common interests. He'd been doing the zine as long as me, even longer, but it was real and good, and it challenged me to step up my game. It made me take what I was doing more seriously. So that helped a lot, and the zine became better because of it.

It became so thick, I couldn't really afford to print it because I only charged fifteen cents. Then it went up a quarter. Eventually it was so thick that it was not cost efficient, and you were just losing money. I didn't want to charge three dollars or something crazy. Eventually it sort of dug itself into a hole from writing too much.

## Why did you get into art?

Cowgill: Neil Blender's skateboard was one thing I liked a lot.[2] It was not rendered incredibly well, but the concept was cool and interesting, and it had emotion. I started tampering with the idea that you could relay emotion without having to be a photographic-style artist. Mark Gonzales—another skateboarder—was similar to that as well. I just started giving it a shot and I really loved it. The first painting I did was a dude with long hair that had nails in his forehead, blood, just something really ridiculous. I put it outside of a gallery with a trash bag covering it, and they put it up in the gallery. I never said whose it was. When I started out, I just used black and white. Every time I sold a painting I would add another color, so eventually I had a full palette.

## Did you ever go to school for art or are you self-taught?

Cowgill: I never took any real classes. Well, that's not true—I did have a painting class at Washington High School. Coach Simpson was my art teacher. He'd always say, "Cowgill, that's a darn fine painting." But most of my painting time has been spent alone in my room for years, figuring it out.

## What would you say is the meaning behind your artwork?

Cowgill: It depends on the painting. Like, there's one up on the wall right here. It's a penguin on a huge circular pad of ice in the middle of nowhere, and he's looking up at the gray clouds and the ice is cracking. It's called "What the Fuck?" His eye color is a light ochre, and he's looking at the cloud up in the sky. There's a little tiny dot of ochre light in the sky. Meaning, there's just a little glimmer of hope in this particular one. But most of the stuff isn't that literal.

## Okay. What do you do now?

Cowgill: Well, I still paint, but not as often because I need glasses. I'm a stage manager at the Great American Music Hall,[3] so I work with

---

2 Neil Blender was a pro skateboarder whose oil paintings were featured on his signature boards.

3 A large, longstanding independent music venue in San Francisco.

bands, which is what I love to do. In Pensacola I was promoting shows, and booking most of the shows for a good amount of time. It's great to be involved in that industry again, and doing the same thing but actually doing it for a living. Back then I gave all the money to the bands, I never took a dime. I had very cheap rent, and before that I was living with my grandmother, so I didn't need to take any money out. I didn't even know you were supposed to, really.

**Do you still consider yourself part of the punk scene?**

Cowgill: Oh, definitely, yeah. Work takes up a lot of my time, but when I do have time I try to get involved. There's a newer generation that's doing cool stuff, and I don't always know what everybody's doing. A lot of those kids I don't know anymore because they're kids. But they're doing good stuff.

# Terry Johnson

"You learn a lot about yourself
when you live with a lot of people"

**To begin with, what is your name and when were you born?**

Johnson: Terry Johnson. November 11, 1961.

**Where were you born?**

Johnson: Sacramento, California.

**Is that where you grew up?**

Johnson: No, my dad was in the Air Force so we moved around a lot. I lived in Japan for a while, stayed in California for a while, spent some time in Boston, and then my parents divorced. That's when I moved to Florida, which was in my middle school years. Essentially, I grew up in Pensacola.

**So, your parents divorced. Tell me a little bit more about your parents.**

Johnson: My dad is from New York City. He was the son of European immigrants. His mom was Irish, his dad was German. She was Catholic, he was Protestant. Their parents wouldn't let them marry. It's the American origin story for white people. But they came to America and got married and had my dad. He grew up in Brooklyn and then joined the Air Force, and was stationed in Mississippi, where he met my very Southern, very northern Mississippi Delta region mother. They got married and had me and my brother.

**Tell me about your childhood.**

Johnson: Well, there's two eras of growing up. There was the part where my parents were married, which was pretty traditional, and we lived in military housing. Then when my parents divorced and we came to Florida, our lives flip-flopped because my mom was a single mom in the seventies, and it was a different world. There wasn't a lot available for her in terms of assistance, so she worked a lot and me and my brother were on our own. Through our high school years we didn't have any adult supervision, but we were good kids and we weren't doing wild stuff. We went to a lot of shows and concerts. There was a punk club back then called McGuigan's Speakeasy—in the seventies, if you can imagine that—and we would just hang out there all the time.

**Where did you go to school?**

Johnson: I went to Escambia High School, and I got there right when the race riot happened in '76.[1] That was my introduction to Southern living. For the most part, my early years were in Boston, which was a super white area, and then coming to the South, and not having any background history of race relations or the problems that the South had suffered through—and then I just walked into a race riot, which was mind-blowing for me. You know, I had *no* idea what was happening.

Escambia High School was kind of wild then. My freshman year was the big race riots, and then the rest of my years there it was on lockdown. We had to go through metal detectors to get into school, and there were huge meetings trying to solve the race issues. It was a very interesting slice of the public-school history of Pensacola because at the same time there were race riots at Pensacola High School as well.

**Did those race riots impact you in your adult life?**

Johnson: Oh, definitely. It definitely influenced the Pipe Bomb records. It was the subject of most of our songwriting, and most of my interests in American history have been black history and race relations. It was *really* impactful.

**That's amazing. I actually had no idea about that, so I'm glad you brought that up. Are you married today?**

Johnson: I've never married Ashley Krey, but he's been my partner for the last seventeen years.

---

1  Race riots broke out at Escambia High School between the years 1972 and 1977 over the use of Confederate imagery. The worst violence took place on February 5, 1976, when thirty students were injured and four shot, including the school's quarterback.

**Do you have any children?**

Johnson: Nope. Just one angry cat, she's sitting staring at me right now.

**Tell me a little bit more about how you got into the punk community.**

Johnson: My brother and I, basically being born at the right time, were teenagers when the Lower East Side punk scene was starting, and the Sex Pistols had just started, and the punk movement in the UK, and Hermosa Beach and the hardcore scene out there were happening. We were ordering records like crazy, and since we had that punk club here in town—strangely—there were punk bands in Pensacola. We just got super into it. Then I went away to school in Birmingham, and Birmingham was a real eye-opener because there were actual big clubs, not dives, that did punk shows. I came back to Pensacola, and I guess it was 1988 when I rented that building on Jefferson Street. My mom had owned a liquor store and a bar, so that was ingrained in me. It seemed natural. I just rented a space and opened up a place called Victor Hugo's. And that's kind of the genesis story for Sluggo's.

**Did you open Sluggo's just because it felt second nature, or was there a secondary reason?**

Johnson: We wanted a place for bands to play. McGuigan's was such a great place, but when that closed the McGuigan brothers started doing punk shows in a room in the back of their dad's bar called Yank's. It was sort of a country-western bar on the west side and would turn into a really weird scene when shows would happen there. The regulars definitely didn't want us there, so having a place that was just a punk bar was the impetus for opening Victor Hugo's.

**What was the environment of Victor Hugo's, and then later Sluggo's?**

Johnson: It was just a little bar area, and then one big room where we did shows. I don't really know how to describe the atmosphere. It was just a punk club.

**What kind of food did you serve?**

Johnson: We didn't serve any food back then.

**Do you serve food now?**

Johnson: Here in Chattanooga? Yeah, Sluggo's is a full-scale vegan restaurant here.[2]

**Awesome. Now we're going to move into your time in the 309 house. How did you first hear about it?**

Johnson: Well, the 309 house didn't exist at the beginning of that story—it starts with a fire. By this point Victor Hugo's had been shut down and I'd opened Sluggo's. Skott Cowgill was a bartender there. There had been a few punkhouses, like the Rat House. Skott lived there, he was in a band called Headless Marines. Jaimes Miller lived there, he was in a band called Distant Silence. And there was a punk scene around all of that. They were two of the bands that played a lot.

Then everyone got kicked out of the Rat House, so Skott moved into an apartment in an old creepy building in North Hill. The place was rundown, unsafe, and one night there was a fire. Skott was trapped in the house and had to jump through a molten window to escape. He was seriously injured, barely alive, and had to be airlifted to a burn unit in Mobile, Alabama.

Jaimes, Rymodee, and I raced to Mobile and just camped there with him for a month. He was in the hospital for a month. His house had burned to the ground and he had lost everything—probably one of the most extensive punk rock record collections that existed at the time. It was a disaster.

He was my best friend, Rymodee's best friend, and Jaimes' best friend, and we were just waiting to find out if he would live. During that time we all made a pact that we were never going to be apart. We were just going to stay together. So on my trips back to Pensacola, because Sluggo's was still open and I was having to drive back and forth, I started searching for a house, and that house at 309 6th Avenue was up for rent. We all talked, and we four were going to move in there and just live out our lives at 309. That was the idea at the time. So that's how the house started.

**How long did you live in the house?**

Johnson: Just the four of us lived there for about three years, and it functioned as a punkhouse. There were shows there, and bands would

---

2  Sluggo's had several incarnations in Pensacola before expanding, and then relocating, to Chattanooga, Tennessee.

come through and stay with us, but we were the only inhabitants. This Bike is a Pipe Bomb formed during that time, those first few years at 309, and then on our first tour, the first time we left town and we were gone for a month, Skott and Jaimes moved these kids, the BMX Bandits, into one of the rooms. After that, more and more people were there all the time. I kept living there for another two or three years. Then Aaron Cometbus was living right next door at 311 and he went on a trip, and I stayed at his house for a while.

**I'm sorry—you broke up a little bit when you said "at 311." Do you mind repeating who you moved in with?**

Johnson: Well, there was a house right next door to 309 that a friend of ours—this punk kid named Rex Ray—had moved into, and we called it Rexico. After Rex moved out, that's where Aaron lived when he moved to town, and Aaron went on a trip. So I moved out of 309 and moved into 311 for a while, and then I left and moved to New Orleans.

**Do you remember the largest amount of people you lived with at one time?**

Johnson: Let's see. So, the BMX Bandits, there were three of them in one room. And, um, let's see—so three, five, six, seven, eight, nine—at one point I would say there were ten of us in there.

**Where did you live in the house? What part of the house?**

Johnson: I lived in every room, except the front room was always Skott's room until he left—that big, giant front bedroom. So I never got to live in there, and I never lived in the upstairs room with the balcony. But I lived in the back bedroom, and the middle bedroom, and the back bedroom upstairs which is completely haunted.

**What was the environment like?**

Johnson: The BMX Bandits were totally wild. They had built all these ramps off the front porch, and when you walked in the door there were stacks of bikes. Me and Rymodee both liked to cook, so we would have these big cooking sessions in the mid-afternoon, and make these giant family meals. There was a lot of beer drinking on the front porch, and everybody had band practice somewhere in the house, so there was a lot of trying to coordinate and not infringe on anyone else.

And then when Rex was next door we were always trying to create contests with the other punkhouses in town—like the "house band feud," where everybody had to start a band and there was a big showdown. That's how the Blank Fight started playing. It was just super creative and rowdy, a great spot for being creative. We also had this, um, recipe that we called "murder soup." We would make a giant pot of soup but make it as *hot* as we could—as many peppers, and make it almost unbearable to eat. Then we would all sit around and struggle to try to eat it.

## What was your bathroom situation?

Johnson: It was terrible, because we only had one bathroom. When there were just four of us it was pretty easy, but as more and more people moved in, it turned into a scheduling issue. We had a big stereo in the bathroom, so you could let people know you were in there having private time or taking a shower by turning on music really loud, and everyone would stay away.

## Could you tell me a little more about the family aspect of 309?

Johnson: Well, in the beginning when it was just Skott and Jaimes and Rymodee and I, there was a super family vibe there. We would have TV nights, and we would all eat together. Skott was recuperating, so we were all in hyper-mothering mode. We pretty much did everything together. Even when the BMX Bandits moved in, and more people started moving in later, although the family vibe wasn't as strong—it was strong in terms of friendship, but just not the regular routine of the house—we would still have activities where we all got together. One time we had this crazy bike ride as a house. We all got on bikes, rode out to Gulf Shores [Alabama], took the ferry over to Dauphin Island, camped on the beach, and rode back the next day. We would do things like that all the time.

## What are some of your fondest memories from living in the house?

Johnson: There's so many. One of my favorite days was Valentine's Day, when me and Rymodee were going to make Valentine's breakfast. We put invitations under everyone's door and told them it was going to be formal, so at 9:00 in the morning everyone came out of their rooms in formal gowns. It was the four of us and the BMX Bandits, and everyone came to the table in thrift store tuxedos and long gowns. Me and Rymodee had taken coat hangers—wire coat hangers—and shaped them into hearts, so we made heart-shaped pancakes, and we had colored the OJ red. We all sat at the big table and we served these beautiful heart-shaped pancakes, and we're halfway through the meal when my boxer, Grendel, comes in and we make him sit under the table. Boxers are kind of notorious for having digestive problems, and apparently he had really bad gas that day [laughs]. He created this smell that literally cleared the room. Everybody just grabbed their plates and ran out of the house.

**That's great. What challenges did you face living in 309?**

Johnson: You learn a lot about yourself when you live with a lot of people. As the number of people grew, you didn't have much alone time. Sitting on the sofa drinking your coffee in the morning, there were people around all the time, and a lot of activity, so you learned to find quiet places inside yourself. I started cherishing moments alone in my room late at night. But I was also overcoming a lot of OCD aspects of my personality—giving in to the fact that things are going to be messy and aren't going to be scheduled just when you want them to be. You're going to bring your stuff to the bathroom and find out you can't get in there for an hour. You learn to overcome it and be creative. "Oh, the bathroom's full? I'm going to ride my bike to Circle K and pee." It was a great experience in terms of getting over myself.

**Was that different from everywhere else you've lived?**

Johnson: This is a crazy thing at my age, but a year ago the last of our roommates moved out of our house here in Chattanooga, and we didn't get new ones. Ashley and I live in a house by ourselves, and this is the first time in my life that I've lived without roommates since before 309. I'm just living with my partner for the first time.

**Why did you leave the house?**

Johnson: You know, I was renting Sluggo's, and Sluggo's in Pensacola had always been a struggle. There were always various forces trying to shut it down, and at that time a new landlord had bought the building and she raised the rent super high. I got offered a bartending job in New Orleans, and I knew I could make a bunch of money. Essentially, I was just going to work in New Orleans to keep Sluggo's open. That's basically it. I'm not sad about that. New Orleans was a great experience, but that's essentially why I left Pensacola, and left 309.

**Are you involved in music today?**

Johnson: M-hm. Right now I'm in a band called River's Edge. I play bass in that band, and we tour a lot. We've done three records and we're going out for a West Coast tour in three weeks. I'm in another band, which is kind of my dream come true—I'm finally in a band with a bunch of ladies. We're called Pleezure Management, and I play drums in that band.

**Are you working on any creative projects that may have begun in, or are supported by, 309?**

Johnson: I would say that all of my projects are based on 309 because that's where I first started to play music, and most of my personal creative process is about music. That's where I learned to write songs, coming up with melodies in my head and then humming them into a guitar tuner and seeing what key they were in, then writing the music from that. All of that was born at 309. Because there was so much encouragement for the idea that anyone can be a songwriter, and everyone was there to help, I would say that it was all born right there.

# Ryan "Rymodee" Modee

### "We were used to living in squalor"

**To begin, where were you born?**

Modee: I was born in Portsmouth, Virginia. I was a Navy brat, so I moved to Pensacola when I was two months old. I was between there and Guantanamo Bay almost all of my childhood.

**When you moved here, was it with both parents?**

Modee: Yes, both my parents. My dad was in the Navy. My mom was a seamstress.

**One of your profile descriptions says that you are mega married. Are you still—Do you still have a wife?**

Modee: I do. We're very married, living in San Francisco now. She's a social worker. She's fucking fantastic.

**Do you guys have any children together?**

Modee: No, we don't.

**Did you go to school in Pensacola?**

Modee: I did. Like I said, we were a Navy family, so I grew up three years at a time in Pensacola and three years at a time in Guantanamo Bay, Cuba.

**How was it going to school in Cuba?**

Modee: It was kind of amazing. Whenever I talk about Guantanamo, people forget that it wasn't always an illegal prison, just an illegal military installation. It was just like living on a Navy base anywhere. There were beaches. It was really warm all the time. It was a lot like Florida. It was really beautiful.

They used to let you go back to Guantanamo if you'd been there before—if you were a Navy brat or in the military yourself. But now that it's an illegal prison, that program has ended. It used to be a dream of mine to go back to Gitmo and just hang out on the beach there for a week or so. No longer, but hopefully I'll make it to the mainland.

**How were you first introduced to the punk scene?**

Modee: I was fourteen in 1984, and I was a little nerdy metal dude, really into hair metal and whatever rock tapes my dad had. I had just returned from Cuba. It was a new school, and I didn't know very many people. I don't remember how I got involved on the swim team, but I did, and there was one punk dude there. He immediately loaned me his records and we started going to shows, and my mind was blown by this friendship and camaraderie. Now it seems so small, but back then it was this giant all-encompassing thing where people from all over the city, who knew things that nobody else did, would meet at these weird bars that turned into all-ages clubs for the night. I just kind of happened upon it.

**Do you still talk to that friend that introduced you?**

Modee: Yeah, his name is Joe Doucette, and every now and then I remind him that it's all his fault. But I'm very thankful for it.

**How were you first introduced to the 309 House?**

Modee: I think it was '95—I'm not positive on the year—but our friend Skott was involved in a pretty bad house fire. We were all quitting our jobs and going over to Mobile to the burn unit to take care of him. We would stay there for nights on end, weeks on end, and then when he was able to leave the hospital, we brought him back home to Pensacola. We put him in a B&B for a week. Then we heard there was this weird house where all the kids were moving out. It wasn't nice, but it was two stories. It was downtown and the rent was super cheap, and we were all pretty busted broke. We knew one or two of the kids there. Even though they weren't punks, we would see them at shows every now and then. We were like, "Great, for a hundred bucks a month there's this killer house that Skott can recover in."

**Was he the first one to move in, or did you move in with him?**

Modee: Skott and I moved in, and I believe Terry Johnson was next. It just exploded after that.

**How was the neighborhood when you first moved in?**

Modee: We were always living in the downtown area, so it wasn't much different. It was just a working-class black neighborhood. The bars we would go to were all walking distance. Waffle House was really close by. Anything you wanted was just right there, so it was kind of perfect.

**Was that one of your big reasons for staying in that house?**

Modee: That, and the rent. At one point we had eleven people there all paying thirty-three dollars a month rent. So we could work one or two days a week, or go on tour, or just hustle and find the rent, and it was never a big deal. Even by 1995 standards, thirty-three dollars a month was pretty easy to come across.

**Were you in contact with the landlord a lot?**

Modee: That was another part of it. I would hate to say he didn't care about the house, but I think he had—I don't remember if it was at the time or maybe just in later years, but he had this pride in support-ing an alternative counterculture. When we paid the rent on time and weren't getting the cops called on us, I think he was kind of stoked on his involvement.

**Were the cops called a lot?**

Modee: I don't know if they were called more than on other groups of people. I think I'm just used to the cops being called a fair amount. We had shows at the house, and this wasn't just 309—everywhere I lived in Pensacola eventually became the place where we'd throw shows. When I was younger there were cops coming to get underage kids, ac-cused runaways. There was loud music well past any decent hours.

**When you were in the house, was it the band This Bike is a Pipe Bomb you were playing with?**

Modee: Yeah, This Bike is a Pipe Bomb formed at that house.

**Were all the members living there when it formed?**

Modee: No, me and Terry were the only people in the band that lived there. At certain times, though, when we were first starting, we had very strange incarnations where some of the members of the house played keyboards and stuff.

**How long did you live in the house?**

Modee: [Sighs] It's hard to say. From '95 to 2006 I was there, for the most part. I finally up and moved in with Jen Knight, but even then I had to move back into 309 after we had a breakup.

**Since you were one of the original members and you had a lot of people moving in and moving out, what was the selection process like?**

Modee: Now, if I had a roommate, I would wonder what kind of job they had, or ask their old roommates how they were as people. Then, there was nobody that really cared what job you had, what skills you had, how clean you were. No one cared about who your past partners were or asked any pertinent information. It was just, would you want to live with them? Space was never an issue. God, there were nooks and crannies all over the house. People would take a nook, people would take a hole, people would take a closet, people would take a couch. Someone even moved his van onto the property and lived in his van in the yard.

**Is there one area in the house you preferred the most?**

Modee: Yeah, the top room overlooking the street, with the balcony.

**Was that the biggest room in the house?**

Modee: No, the biggest room was probably what was most of the time Skott's room, which was the very first room when you walked in the door. The top room is kind of weird in size, the main part of it was small and the ceilings were low, but it had spaces everywhere. It was like three different compartments, and then the view from the balcony. You could play guitar on the balcony and never bother anyone— or probably bother someone, but nobody said anything. You could be up till 4:00 in the morning, sitting on the balcony with a cool breeze. There are secret compartments, little hidden compartments in there. It satisfied a bunch of childish fort dreams.

**Can you walk me through like a typical day there?**

Modee: I don't know what would be typical. I definitely had the leisure of waking up at whatever hour I wanted. The kitchen was filled with cast iron, and although it was a disgusting mess there was plenty of food and stuff to use. I would usually get up and make either spaghetti or mashed potatoes and gravy, or a pizza, for breakfast. I would have one or two band practices a day. We would end up at Whataburger or Waffle House or the bookstore, or go to the beach. And depending on what year it was we could either go to a CORE[1] meeting, or some activist meeting, or have a protest. There would be a show at the house. I would go to work at Sluggo's running sound, and then I would go to bed at 4:00 in the morning.

**You mentioned the mess that was part of the house. Was that ever a big challenge for you living there?**

Modee: The mess?

**The mess.**

Modee: No, it wasn't for me. I think I've made leaps and strides in my adult years, but I'm kind of a slob in general, and definitely have been okay with clutter. Yeah, it never bothered me at all. No, I was kind of into it. Occasionally it would get pretty gross and we'd all agree, "Oh yeah, some shit needs to get done." But we all kind of grew up—at least the core group—used to living as poor, pretty sloppy individuals.

**Other members have talked about fleas in the house. Was that ever a known problem?**

Modee: Yes [laughs]. But when we moved into the house, those guys were worse than we were. I thought hanging at all these punkhouses I was used to some bad shit. One guy, we hadn't seen in a month. We were like, "Is that guy coming back? I don't think so, let's throw his shit out." I went in and immediately got devoured by fleas. It got so bad, one night I woke up and I couldn't take it anymore. There was some flea and tick shampoo in the refrigerator, so I went and took a shower with flea and tick shampoo so I could go back to bed, and that was the first good night of sleep I had in a while.

**Oh no, that sounds a little difficult to deal with.**

Modee: I don't want to romanticize it in any way, but we were kind of used to living in squalor. Looking back now, I'm like, "Oh fuck, that's gross," but back then it was just part of living in a punkhouse. We never had scabies [laughs]. Having fleas at that time didn't seem like a big deal.

**Compared to the other punkhouses that you lived in, how was 309? Did it stand out as different?**

Modee: You know, I've always been pretty naive or innocent when it comes to hard drug use, especially in Pensacola. And I've been fortu-

---

1  Collective of Resource Empowerment, a community center founded by 309 residents.

nate that it never really hit me. I never saw it at the houses I lived in, in Pensacola. We were fortunate that we were a small town and we were all pretty good, for the most part. We all had a large chunk of our childhood spent together, and we were all pretty tight.

**I just need a little clarification. You're saying 309 was better than the other houses you've been in when it came to drug use.**

Modee: Again, I'm pretty naive, so if anything happened, I didn't see it. But traveling around with my bands I have seen some punkhouses and some punk towns that were ravaged by heavy drug use, and that was something that made me want to stay in Pensacola. We had many opportunities to leave Pensacola—not just for the band but for any number of reasons, we could have just picked up and said, "Fuck this tiny Navy town." But we were lucky that we were all really good friends, a pretty tight-knit community, and we didn't have fucking needles or spoons underneath people's beds.

**Was there a lot of drinking going on?**

Modee: Oh, yes. Absolutely. I mean, depending on what year. Pensacola had a weird romanticism with straight edge that I dabbled in until I was thirty. I didn't drink at all, and almost anyone I was friends with had at least a year or two where they were straight edge, and years where they were the complete opposite of straight edge—even myself.

**So why did you ultimately decide to leave the house?**

Modee: I was dating Jen Knight and she bought a house. Yeah, I moved in with my girlfriend. I could turn that into a nice or an ugly story, but I think I'll just leave it at that.

**Did 309 have any effect on you professionally or personally?**

Modee: I learned how to live communally. I'm a pretty bad communicator, so I'd hate to think what my communication skills would be if I wasn't forced to live with eleven-to-fifteen people at a time. It helped me to communicate, even though my communication skills are pretty piss poor even now.

**You mentioned that you were part of some activist activities around town. Did those ideas originate in the house?**

Modee: I mean, we were teenagers in the mid-eighties, and what we call "activism" was just going to a protest, or having a protest. I can't say that originated at 309.

**Were there any causes that really stuck out that you involved yourself in?**

Modee: Well, pre-309, the Klan would actually come to Pensacola fairly often, and we would protest that in disgust, and couldn't believe it was an outfit that still existed. I'm not sure how old you are, but you know Pensacola is where the abortion bombings happened? I'm sure there are still giant billboards, anti-abortion billboards. We were always in favor of women's rights or abortion rights. Those two, for me anyway, were the main thing: protesting against racism and for women's rights.

**What are your thoughts on the 309 Museum?**

Modee: I go back and forth. I'm a little leery of romanticizing the past. I'm leery of people pretending we were something that we weren't. But I'm also a hoarder and I'm really into the past, so part of me is excited. So, I'm critical but excited.

**I think this project speaks a lot about the environment in Pensacola growing up and what was going on.**

Modee: Yes. I still have such a soft spot for that era of Pensacola because I grew up there. It's a Navy town, it's conservative, it's beach. It's in the middle of nowhere, no one wants to visit it, but at the same time we had every punk band that's ever been worth a shit come through there. There we were, all these redneck punks who were really fortunate to have that influence. We had all our favorite bands from all these tiny little communities that we loved coming to us, and it made for something really magical. We weren't Atlanta or New Orleans, we were Pensacola. But we got to see all this stuff, and have a great skate scene and a great BMX scene, and—I hate to say that we didn't deserve it, but I felt like we lucked upon it, maybe.

**Is there one memory that sticks out the most?**

Modee: This memory has probably been told and retold. It's when we were all becoming vegan and learning how to cook together. At that time, there was no place to eat if you wanted to be vegan, so we were like, "Why don't we make the house into a restaurant?" We just put up flyers that said, "Hey, next Tuesday 309 is going to be a restaurant for lunch." And we did it. It was weird, but there were times when we had a line out the door, and it was all bar people, neighborhood people, people who weren't vegetarians, and people who went into our disgusting house who sat and ate with us and were pretty stoked on having this weird restaurant happen in a punkhouse. That's where I started to take my cooking pretty seriously. That was an important moment for me.

**Do you do anything with your cooking now?**

Modee: Not any longer. Up until four years ago I was a sous-chef at a vegan, gluten-free, organic restaurant, and it was fantastic. I'll be fifty this year, and I think the kitchen—the life of a kitchen worker—is for a younger person. I've got a pretty cool job now. I work at a collectively run, vegetarian grocery store. I'm still involved with vegan food. I'm pretty thankful for my time in kitchens. It was a great run, but I'm also super stoked to be out of them.

# Gabe Smith

"We always took it over
the top, every day"

This interview was conducted at Hula Moon Tattoo Studio. Thank you, Gabe, for letting us come into your personal space.

Smith: I live with people in my personal space.

**Okay.**

Smith: When you tattoo somebody, you're in their bubble, but they're also in yours. You smell their bad breath, you feel their sweat and their bodily fluid. When I get home, I don't want anyone in my bubble. But while I'm here, pop them bubbles. Do it.

**Awesome. So we're going to start with some simple questions first. Could you state your full name?**

Smith: Famous Gabe.

**Where were you born?**

Smith: Meridian, Mississippi.

**Did you live there your entire life?**

Smith: I lived there until I got done with high school and then slowly migrated out. I've been all over.

**When did you make it down to Pensacola?**

Smith: My mom moved here in the early nineties, and that's when I first got in touch with the quote-unquote Pensacola scene. I was on a break from school and came and lived with my mother because I wanted some quiet time to write. I met some punk rocker kids who were putting on shows, making zines, and doing all the dumb shit you do when you're punk rock. Then I moved away. I was up in Wisconsin for a while, then I moved down here in 1996.

**Can you tell me a little bit about your parents?**

Smith: Sure, my mom is super awesome. She lives next door to me to this day. If you've ever seen the *Downtown Crowd,* my mom works for them. My mom sells advertisement. She could sell a legless man crutches if she really believed he needed them. My father was a pretty amazing man. He was a jack-of-all-trades. He performed at the Grand Ole Opry. He did civil rights stuff. He taught us that to judge people is wrong, and let us be free to experiment with ourselves and be punk rock before we knew what punk rock was.

**Where were they born?**

Smith: Meridian, Mississippi.

**So you all moved down together?**

Smith: No, no. My parents divorced when I was right out of high school. That's when my momma moved down here. My dad, he lived out the rest of his days in Meridian.

**Do you have any siblings?**

Smith: Yes, I do. I have a couple of brothers and sisters. I have a bunch of half-brothers and sisters that I don't talk to. I have a sister that lives here in town. I've got two amazing brothers. One of them works for a BMX bicycle fabrication company and the other one ended up in the *Guinness Book of World Records* and is also the host of *Stan Lee's Super-humans* on the History Channel.

**Cool!**

Smith: I can't help what my brothers did. I'm a man on my own, but I do attribute it to my father. My father was very proactive. I wanted to draw, and he bought me drawing stuff. My brother, he wanted to weld. "Here, let me show you how to do that." My other brother's a contortionist. My dad goes, "Here's books on contortionism and Houdini and people doing these weird things in India." He just pushed us to do what we wanted. He used to say that if you do what you love to do, you don't care if you live in a box.

**Were you close to your siblings at all?**

Smith: Yes, of course. When you grow up, you grow up with all of your family. Me and my brothers are probably way more tight. I feel bad that I'm not close with my sister, but we are on different highways. But me and my BMX brother, we're inseparable. Originally, wherever I lived, he lived. I got my foot in the door, then he just came in the next day and never left. We've always been together.

**Where did you go to school?**

Smith: In Mississippi. I went to high school and college up there. I've only been to Mississippi schools. Other than the school I went to up in Wisconsin, but I don't count that.

**Do you have any special memories from your childhood that you want to share?**

Smith: Not to be a Negative Nelly, but it's terrible when you love where you live but you don't love the people that live there. That was Mississippi. I love the land, I love the dirt, I love the country. But I never had a group to fit into, I always knew I was different. Me and my younger brothers, we were the only kids in town that had mohawks or weird haircuts. People would lose their minds. My brother got kicked out of school because he went to school with his mohawk up. It's what punks did, but nobody's ever seen that before, so they don't know.

**Do you think not fitting in influenced you to join the punk scene?**

Smith: Absolutely. To me, Pensacola was really the first punk scene. In Mississippi there were punk rockers and there were shows, but they were so limited and far between. If you were punk rock in Mississippi, you were driving to New Orleans at least. We'd drive quite a bit to go to punk shows—here and Mobile, but mostly Pensacola. Sluggo's had this answering machine that would tell you what was going on.

**Can you tell me your earliest memories of 309?**

Smith: How it went was, I wasn't intending to move to Pensacola. My brother was over in Fort Walton Beach working for this guy who had a BMX company, and I was on my way from Wisconsin. I had this Volkswagen '74 and it broke down at the Cracker Barrel out on the interstate here. I called someone up I'd met a few years earlier. "Hey, man, is it cool to crash at your house until I get my van going?" So I got my van towed out there, and I'd work on it. I got a job at Bikes Plus. But I was riding my bicycle from Tiger Point down Navy Boulevard and back every day. It was a really long haul on a bike, plus the people I was living with, I think I'd worn out my welcome. I got stuck in this thing where I started sleeping downtown with the homeless dudes because I didn't want to ride all the way back.

I'd met Skott Cowgill before at Sluggo's. I'd go down to the pub and hang out with him. He said, "We've got a room for rent if you want." Skott, he was a good host. I think he was hustling me to pay his rent, too, but I was like, "Screw it, man. I've got the money." So I moved into 309. The problem was, three quarters of the house was on tour with their bands. They came home and I was sitting on the couch.

They were like, "Who the hell are you?"

And I was like, "Who the hell are *you*? You're in my house!"

But I was in their house, as a matter of fact. As soon as I met these people, you knew right away we were going to be best friends, and we still are, for the most part.

**What did the house look like when you were there?**

Smith: It was the ultimate level of chaos in control. Skott Cowgill, Terry Johnson who owned Sluggo's, Rymodee from This Bike is a Pipe Bomb, and Jaimes Miller—those guys were the core of the house. But I think they hadn't lived there very long because when I went in my room, which was upstairs in the back, it was so nasty. There were corked bottles with cigarette butts in them. There were the worst porno mags you could imagine just randomly strewn about the room. Being a tattooer, I had plenty of gloves, and I put them on and went to work cleaning the room up. It was from the people who lived in the house before us—the original drunk punks of Pensacola. They were in the house first, so I feel like we were second gen, but the second gen is what made the house popular. Because we had one of the most influential punk bands from the Southeast living there for years. They paved the way, so they put it on the map.

I feel like after we left, the house got more crazy. When I lived there, we had schedules. There were schedules! We had a house class which someone would teach. We had sports activities the whole house had to be at. Your only excuse for not joining activities was work.

**Really?**

Smith: Yeah. We'd always have lunch and dinner together. We did everything together, the whole house. We went on bike rides together. One of my favorite things, my favorite memories from the house, was drunk darts. Drunk darts was where we'd have this dart board downstairs, and you would do trick shots that were very dangerous. There were a few who would skateboard down the staircase throwing darts.

**That sounds hilarious.**

Smith: That's the parts of the house that I miss. I miss the group part of it. But, you know, every spring has to have a fall.

**Leading into that, can you talk about the challenges of living in the house?**

Smith: I think my biggest challenge was coming from Mississippi, man. I had this sense of how ideal punk was. "This punk rock, it's amazing! This is where I belong." Me and my brother used to go crazy. We were the guys who were naked, doing flips off the stage. We just didn't care. We always took it over the top, every day—that's how we lived. We'd go out, and we'd think, "We're going to go to the Fireside Bowl in Chicago where some real punk rock people will be." Then you realize we're still the craziest motherfuckers there. Just two old dumb redneck boys from Mississippi who found their way to this beautiful thing.

I think that the biggest challenge is when you look back. There was no challenge when I lived there, but when you look back you start to see through some of the smoke and mirrors. There was a romanticism about it, and there was the reality too. There were people cheating on their girlfriends, people doing drugs. It was really a climate of getting crazy, sometimes to the point of excess. It wasn't really the best thing ever. I watched people who I think suffered mental illness who should've taken proper channels to get help, but instead they medicated themselves through the bad times.

That's always it: hindsight is 20/20. Overall, I'll rate it as one of the great experiences of my life, but I also have a wonderful kid and a wonderful wife now. Those are my glory days, today.

**Can you elaborate on that, and why you think it was romanticized?**

Smith: I mean, I get it. But that's where the reality comes in. You've got all of these kids who were clamoring to help save 309. "Let's clean it up. Let's paint it, make it look good. Make it a model of the neighborhood." But for twenty-five years it was the complete polar opposite of that. It was loud. There was no respect to the neighbors over noise. Kids drank on the porch. I was one of them!

Now I've owned my own business here in Pensacola for twenty years, and I've gotten to know the neighbors we had then. In a weird way, I felt compelled to apologize for my behavior. These were people who moved out of the neighborhood because of that house. They'd be like, "Oh, cool, those kids are moving out. Oh no, there's somebody else!"

**It sounds pretty chaotic at times. Could you walk us through a typical day at 309?**

Smith: When I lived there, me and my brother were a little bit of early birds. We would get up and go ride bikes in the morning when it was cool and then come home. By that time, everybody would be waking up. We'd always cook together. That was a big thing. For a lot of us, especially the vegan kids, we became vegan together. We learned that process of cooking and experimenting. I remember when Ever'man [Natural Foods] was just a little tin hut and it didn't have a lot of shit. It wasn't all of this prefabricated vegan food. Now you can get anything vegan. Then, you had to make your own stuff.

That was a big part of the afternoon. We always had designated times. I can't remember if it was Skott or Rymodee who made this chart of what day and what we'd have to do. We'd have art time and make stuff. We'd go for a walk. We loved to put pennies on the train tracks for the trains to run over and squish, and we'd make stuff out of those. I told you about the drunk darts, but we'd also have crazy basketball. Somebody would pick you up and dunk you into the garbage can, and you'd throw the ball out of the garbage can. It was quite a sight to see.

Most of the house worked at either the Handlebar or Sluggo's, so we'd all go to work together. Then we'd go to the other bar together. When we'd go to the Waffle House, we'd take up two or three booths when the whole house was there.

I tell people all the time, if you're not married, even if you have a significant other, why the fuck would you pay a thousand dollars a month to live in an apartment by yourself? That is so stupid. Do you want to know how we went around the world doing all this crazy traveling? It's because we had eleven people in the house. I think I paid nine hundred dollars a *year* to live in 309. So all the money I made went to traveling. That was the beauty of it. There would be times when the house would get lonely, there would only be four people when you're used to having more than ten.

**When did you leave?**

Smith: When my son was born. That's when I moved out.

**Is that the reason you left, because of your son?**

Smith: Yeah. I met Jordie's mom. It was a one-night stand. She got pregnant. I knew that I wanted to be a dad. You don't know until it happens to you. Until it happens, you're like, "I'm never having kids." I was almost thirty when it happened. "Whoa, this is cool. This is what I was meant to do."

That's why I left. Who wants to wake up to a screaming ass baby? Everyone else is coming home and you're getting up with the kid. It didn't seem like the life I wanted to live at the time, so I moved upward toward the East Hill area and lived with Terry Johnson and Dave Myers. So the reality was that Terry Johnson left before I did. I remember Terry had this dog named Grendel. That was the toughest part about moving out, not having Grendel. I'll tell you a little Grendel story.

**Go for it.**

Smith: So like I said, I'm a tattooer. I always have the proper gloves laying around the house. They were very useful because Grendel loved to eat anything. He'd eat the sofa, I'm not even kidding. We would go to a thrift store, get him a sofa. It would take about a month, but he'd chew the arms off, the backs off—whatever. He would just destroy. Of course panties, those were a delicacy. Socks. We'd come home and he's all hunched up. So you'd put on a glove, reach back and pull the old butt floss out, and there you'd go!

So one day, we come home and Grendel's all hunched up and crying. And I'm like, "I got it, I got it." I put the glove on and reached back, but when I started pulling on it, it was like a little zip line—and Grendel took off running. He gets about ten feet away from me, and I realize this is a pair of pantyhose. So it pops out of his ass and slings shit all over my face and chest. At 309, we didn't have no A/C or nothing, and there were never any screens on the windows. There were always bugs flying around. So I literally turned to the open window and projectile vomited out the window. Those were the good old days.

**[Laughs] I have to contain myself. So what does "punk" mean to you?**

Smith: See how stupid you can be [laughs]. I don't know, man. I thought I knew what it meant. You know, it means whatever you want it to mean. Everything is organic, which is another reason I was like, "Why are you guys saving 309? It was supposed to die." If it's dead, it's dead—that's the meaning of punk rock. Punk rock is not nostalgia. It's always about the immediacy of the day. That's the carpe diem, if you will: live in the moment.

When we used to go to Sluggo's, you'd see some super crusty punk kids with spikes on their jackets. But, oh, here are some mod guys. And here's a dude who looks all rockabilly. Here's a goth kid. They all went to Sluggo's because there was nowhere else for them to go. There were so many different genres that came together and that fit together. It was very welcoming. It was a cool place. I remember everyone had their little spot: the gothy kids hung out at the library and the crusty punks hung out at the bar. Then there were the scenester kids who would be up in the pool table room playing air hockey.

But then the punk scene started to get more narrow. It's very narrow now. It got so that the crustier you were, the dirtier you were, the less hygienic you were, the better you fit in. No punk rocker would've ever left the house without a black T-shirt on, but all of a sudden kids were wearing white T-shirts. They wanted to be like, "We're not mall punkers." Do you know why they wore the white T-shirts? So you could see how dirty they were. Look, if you're going to go out of your way to dress a certain way, you might as well shop at the Gap. Who cares, you know? I guess my style is called "free." I'll wear shit until the cows come home, man. I'm cheap, like a bird in the morning.

But all that stuff's backfired on me, too. Like that whole trainhopping kid thing. Whatever! I remember this one time at Subterranean Books. There was a big jar for Books for Prisoners, maybe it had a hundred bucks in it. These trainhopping kids come in. They're like, "Hey, can we stash our bags here while we go panhandle?" Sure, man. So that afternoon when these hobo kids come back, they stole the jar of money. I feel like I've kind of been ostracized from my punk rock community because I started being more outspoken about certain things. But of course they called me up. They want a little brawn with their brains. They were like, "Hey, umm, we're going to try and get these guys. We know where they're at."

I said, "Well, you know what? Call it one hundred dollars tuition towards the School of Hard Knocks. Because you're going to get in a fight. One of those kids is going to stab you. How much is the hospital bill going to be? Or better yet, they run off. You're going to come open up the bookstore in the morning—you know how much it's going to cost to replace that glass? Maybe next time you shouldn't trust people that you don't know. Sorry, man."

Again, the romanticism of it, and that was the reality. Since they couldn't get me, they got my friend. I won't use his name, but I'll call him by his nickname, Ugly Knuckles. He just walked up and pulled a gun on them and told them to get out of town.

The bookstore people were like, "Oh god, no."

Well, don't call on the help if you don't know who the help is.

**Do you think the romanticism is what saw your involvement with the punk scene change?**

Smith: No, I think it just had to do with being a parent. When you have a kid, you can get all holy rolly, but who's going to feed your kid? You are. If you ain't got food, how you going to feed your kid? That becomes every waking moment. You become obsessed. All these things I was so passionate about kind of went out the window.

I just wanted to be a dad, and I feel like I've done an okay job with it, but it pushed me away from a lot of things. I still enjoy going to shows. Sometimes I feel like I'm the old guy at the shows. I remember going, "Look at that guy, he's old and he's at the show." Now I'm that guy. But it is what it is.

**So, tattooing. When did you originally get interested in tattooing?**

Smith: It was definitely when I was a kid. Me and my brother, we were always on our BMX bikes. We used to ride down to the Harley shops with some dude who rode motorcycles, but he also tattooed out at his place. My brother was like, "Bro, we should cut grass, save up money, and get one of these kits and we could learn how." He wanted to learn. He wanted to tattoo more than I did, but I was the artsy one, so I got pushed into it. Next thing you know, one thing led to another and me and my brother got in a fight with an entire fraternity. We were bruisers back then. We liked brawling, I guess. So we were fighting this little fraternity, and it got pretty hairy for about twenty or thirty seconds. All of a sudden, everyone starts screaming. The local tattoo guy had just driven by, saw a big fight going down and thought, "Oh, those guys are cool." He pulled a bat out and went into the crowd to try to get to us. He had ten dudes jump on him. I think he got his face cut up on the bumper of a car. He had to get stitches. Shit like that. Pretty gnarly. But after that, we got to be friends. I loved tattooing and went through the motions apprenticeship-wise.

**Did you do your apprenticeship here?**

Smith: No, this was in Mississippi. This was the wild days when you had to go to the damn sewing store. What's the sewing store everyone goes to?

**Joann's?**

Smith: Joann's. Someone would go to Joann's fabric store and buy all of the number twelve sewing needles. Then you'd get a pair of snips and you'd snip all the ends off them, and make your needles from scratch. It was a wild ride. And I love it. I can't explain the attraction of it. It's an addictive thing to do.

**Did your time living in 309 influence your art or style?**

Smith: I was already painting a lot before I moved into 309, but being surrounded by people that were also making art, we all fed off of each other. I remember when Skott Cowgill did his very first painting, and now he's done thousands of paintings. Again, there was that financial freedom. I wouldn't say that it influenced me in a certain way, because what you were doing wasn't finding your art but finding yourself. But through finding yourself, you find your art. Does that make sense?

**Yes. Do you have any crazy tattoo stories you want to tell us?**

Smith: Oh, yes. They all involve Rymodee, of course. I remember we were about to tattoo at the house one night, and it was hot as balls. So we went out on the porch, and I tattooed Rymodee's stomach on the front porch of 309. I remember because we were right next to the 311 house. That's where Aaron Cometbus and them lived.

Then everyone got the 309 keys tattooed on them. I tattooed Rymodee's in the sound booth while he was doing sound for a show at Sluggo's. There was no light, so I was holding a mag light in my mouth while tattooing on him. We were laughing so hard, but I did a box, and then I would do the key. Those were freehand, but when I put the last line down to connect the box I totally missed it by a quarter of an inch. So it looks like a box with an opening on it. He was so mad at first, but now he likes it.

Well, let me tell you this: I don't even remember where my 309 tat *is*. [Smith looks for the tattoo on his body]. Oh, there it is. So that's what it was supposed to be. That tattoo is twenty-five years old.

**It looks great still.**

Smith: Well, thank you.

**So are you still associated with the punk scene in Pensacola?**

Smith: Well, there's a guy, and he's probably not going to be happy. I had an altercation at Chizuko[1] with this young man. I think there's a lot kids who get worked up about shit because they want to be a part of something grand. I'm not saying civil rights is fair now or anything like that, but some of these kids would love to go back and be in these grand marches. I think they're romanticizing, not thinking about the reality of all the bullshit that came with them. Our country has come a long way in the past thirty years. Me and my friends were born during the civil rights movement or right after. When you go back to those moments and you transfer them to modern times, you look at how far we've come. I'm not saying we should stop fighting. Doing what's right is always the right thing to do—my dad taught me that. But we should also celebrate how far we've come. I think a lot of people have squandered some opportunities. They're so busy looking at details that they miss the big picture.

**That sounds like a whole other interview that we'll have to get into later.**

Smith: Yeah.

**Are you involved in the revitalizing of 309 into a museum?**

Smith: At first, I didn't know. Yes, I want to support it. But also, being a realist, this is completely ridiculous to pay a bunch of money for a house that really—I mean, who gives a shit who lived there? I put in my two cents. I told them I have contacts in the railroad industry. That house was originally a flophouse for the railroad. The room where I lived, it had all these secret doors from the Prohibition period. I found some really old bottles where people would probably toss them if they got inspected. So you should make the downstairs about the trains and the upstairs, maybe one room, be the history of the 309 house. Because unless you're in that immediate scene, who would care? Gulf Power doesn't care. Who's going to pay the Gulf Power bill? Are you going to charge admission for people to come in? I would never pay to go in the place.

So it was that kind of thing. I just didn't understand. To me, instead of being nostalgic we need to build infrastructure for the homeless.

---

1  A bar/venue opened by former Sluggo's staff.

Let's spend that money on them. Hell, if the private sector wants to get behind it, I'll back it. I just didn't feel like it was the city's responsibility to take care of a house that never gave a shit about its neighborhood until it was threatened. As far as historical? You want to preserve it for history? Punk rock's got nothing to do with this. It's all about the railroad, and the railroad connecting with the seaports. That's what made Pensacola stay here. After all the times it got wiped away, there's still a port. There's still some train tracks, and that's what kept it going. That's what still keeps it going, to be honest.

**Would you say 309 is significant to you still?**

Smith: Yeah, it is. It was a really huge part of my life. I don't squander those memories, I relish them. I have great memories there. It did shape me. I mean, shit, Hula Moon, this is our twentieth year. I modeled Hula Moon after 309. "Let's all get together, get a bunch of roommates, pay the bills, and make it on the cheap." So if you want to go travel as a tattooer you can, and the bills will still get paid. All the money goes into a big pot that pays the bills. That was the same thing at 309. That was the advantage of having all of those people living in the house. I'd have five people living in my room: myself, my brother Dave, Ryan Corrigan, Scott Alvarez who's one of the founding members of Hula Moon, and our friend Katie Bigtoe. She might as well have lived at 309 because she was always over there, crashing out.

**Any other stories you want to add? I know you have so many.**

Smith: The other person I wanted to tell you about was Ryan Corrigan. Ryan's a pretty amazing dude. He builds ramps, skateparks, and stuff. Ryan lived in the house. Ryan's girlfriend is also from the house, Billie Latzer. If punk rock would've had a princess in Pensacola, it would've been Billie Latzer. Billie Latzer still is one of the sweetest, kindest, most beautiful women I've ever known. I will always love her. She's like the best little sister that any person could ever have. She's awesome. She and Ryan met there in 309. They've been in love for sixteen or seventeen years. If Ryan's reading this, he better hurry up and get that ring he's always talking about.

# Jen Knight

"Everything had gravy on it"


**This interview is taking place on the front porch of the 309 punk-house. To begin with, where were you born?**

Knight: I was born in San Diego, California.

**When was that?**

Knight: In 1973. Way back then.

**Did you grow up in San Diego?**

Knight: No, no, I grew up here for the most part. Right after high school I moved to San Francisco, and then I came back in 1996.

**Can you tell me about your parents? Who were they?**

Knight: My father was an Equal Employment Opportunity specialist, and my mother worked in an office on the base. My father worked for the Navy as a lawyer. If somebody were to be fired because of their ethnicity or their gender, he would help fight to get their job back, or compensation.

**Where in Pensacola did you primarily live?**

Knight: Well, I grew up out in Perdido, so in high school I would stay in town with friends a couple days a week. If you're going to a punk show, asking afterwards, "Can you give me a ride home?" is impossible—it's forty minutes away. So I would just stay in town. Then I moved out of my parents' house when I was sixteen and got an apartment by the mall. I worked at Ruby Tuesday in the mall and finished out my high school at PJC [Pensacola Junior College].

**How did you first become involved in the punk scene?**

Knight: I surfed a little and was friends with a bunch of people that skated. I ended up going to the skatepark a lot, and just from hanging out, somebody took me to a couple of shows. I saw the Bad Brains and it blew my mind. I knew I'd found my place. The people were different than your general high school crowd—they were artistic, and didn't give a fuck about what was or wasn't cool. It was just a different mind-set, and I felt like I fit in a little bit better.

**What was the location?**

Knight: It was at the Nite Owl. It was just a bottle club they would let punk bands play at, and this guy, Gus Brandt, would bring in amazing bands and just open our minds. It was really cool because it wasn't such a clique-ish thing. There would be a metal band opening up for a punk band, and all these different kinds of music. Everybody came out to see whatever band it was, it didn't matter if you had friends playing or not.

**Was Gus Brandt in the scene or was he just a promoter?**

Knight: No, he was longtime in the scene. Definitely. You know, this is a small town, so everybody knows each other. There's not really anybody that's some bigwig bringing bands in.

**What were other places you frequented to hear live music of that kind?**

Knight: There was another place called the Mix that was before my time. A little bit later on, Sluggo's was where the Handlebar is now, and a lot of cool stuff came through there. The Replacements played there, Black Flag played there. That was eighteen-and-up, so I'd wear different outfits and costumes and try to sneak in, and listen through the back door where the sound booth was. Every once in a while, they'd open the door and let me watch.

**Can you describe what it looked like inside the Nite Owl?**

Knight: It looked like a dark bar with a stage. Just basically dark. It would be this transition from the regular older crowd that was there, then young kids and skateboards and amplifiers and people loading in from tour vans and just flooding into this venue, cramming to get up front for a couple hours of people screaming at us onstage. It was awesome.

**Can you tell me what the Handlebar was like before the fire?**

Knight: Oh yeah, yeah. I worked at the Handlebar as well. Before the fire, it was this historic space in the punk scene in Pensacola. It went through a couple different transitions and then ended with the Lamars owning it. Jimmy Lamar was in local bands, and his parents bought the bar and continued to have shows. There were a lot of us that had grown up here, and grown up in the scene, that ended up working as bartenders there. We moved away and came back and it was always a home, it was always there. It was always kind of like, I don't want to say a punk *Cheers,* but it was. It could be rowdy, it could be sweet. Somebody threw me a surprise birthday there one time. They're like, "Look, it's all your friends, they're all here!"

"Well my friends are *always* here, what's the—oh, it's my birthday, that's right."

When it burned down, it was really sad. But as the building is smoldering and there's soot in the air, it was amazing how many of us came out with coolers and lawn chairs and beer, and we all sat around like it was a campfire on some very strange camping trip, but with this beautiful sense of community. We all faced the bar and we were toasting it. Everybody's telling stories of their favorite times or, "Remember when that band played?"

Jimmy ran in there. It's all taped off, police tape everywhere. Everybody is like, "No, Jimmy! What are you doing?" He ran in there and he came back out with a flat of PBR that was still cold. It had soot all over it, but it was still cold.

**Did the 309 Punks and the other regulars at the Handlebar do anything special for the Lamar family at the time?**

Knight: Yeah, of course. There were benefits all over the place for the Handlebar. I know that End of the Line had benefits. I can't remember which happened first, but the only reason we started doing more and more shows at the cafe was because Sluggo's had shut down and the Handlebar burned down, and there wasn't any place to do all-ages shows even before that. But up until lately there wasn't any "309 Punks," there were just people that lived here.

**When you think back, are there any shows at those places that stand out?**

Knight: There's so many. Every week you wanted to hear everything, you wanted to absorb everything, you wanted to buy all the records, you wanted to figure out who's crawling out of that stinky van. I went to everything—every single show. I didn't want to miss out on anything.

**Were there any gigs here at 309?**

Knight: Absolutely. There would be people lined up on the staircase. Got to watch out for those splinters, man. Whew! That wooden house. Bands played right in that living room area. But, honestly, there were always people playing guitars and banjos and fiddles and stuff out on the porch.

**Was there different kinds of music being played at the house?**

Knight: Yeah. Depending on what roommates there were at the time, and what kind of band they were in, and who was touring through. But there was always music.

**How did bands get the word out about upcoming shows?**

Knight: Flyers. A lot of flyers. Handing 'em out, and sticking them on phone poles and bulletin boards. A lot of word of mouth.

**Were these flyers handmade?**

Knight: All flyers should be handmade.

**As far as shows at this house, were the police ever called because of the music?**

Knight: Of course they were. But this was predominantly an older neighborhood. Now there's a younger generation of people living here and buying the houses and flipping them. Then it was an older neighborhood, so everybody went to bed early, and there was respect for that. You had to be done by like 10:30 or 11:00, and if not they'll come and shut it down. I mean, we're not trying to give anybody a heart attack.

**What was the neighborhood like when you first got here?**

Knight: Like I said, it was older. It was quiet. It was darker because there were a couple street lights out for years and years. This was before Hurricane Ivan, so we still had the Amtrak that went through a *lot*.[1] That was noisy because they blew their horn if they saw anybody out on the street, or on the porch, or even in front of End of the Line. They just blared their horn like crazy. A couple of the people that lived here had jobs they got up in the mornings for, but the horn would keep them up all night long. They made picket signs and went and stood in

---

1 Amtrak discontinued service to Pensacola in the aftermath of Hurricane Ivan in 2004 and Hurricane Katrina in 2005.

front of the Amtrak and were like, "No More horns! We're trying to sleep."

But the neighborhood itself, there was no uppity, snooty people that really had issue with 309 in the neighborhood. Until Jo Green became the head of the neighborhood association. There was 309, there was End of the Line Cafe, and there was Room 1026, which was a bar down the street that our friend Jason owned, and they had shows there too. And here was somebody that didn't even live in the neighborhood, they just owned a bunch of property here. They lived in Gulf Breeze, but they threw up this *huge* issue and basically wanted everybody out. They tried to create a stink. But look who's all still here!

**This Jo Green character, around what time did he pop up on the scene?**

Knight: She. I think it was a she. And it wasn't like somebody coming to the door. It was just something you get in the mail, kind of cowardly. "I'm going to go to the city!" Instead of personally trying to take care of this, here's a citation.

**What were some good memories of the more DIY places that people would play?**

Knight: Well, Against Me! would come through here a lot. We rented generators and made a bunch of food and drinks and hauled all the stuff down the railroad tracks to Hobo Beach. That was really fun. It was kids hanging in trees, climbing up in the trees, watching the show from above. The sound carrying over the water, it was just beautiful. Setting up a table of food and having the music and all these people. Just this heartwarming sense of community that's something you can't write in a script.

**As far as how you guys would get around to different shows, I read an article in the *Pensacola News Journal*. I think it was when gas prices were high, and it talked about how you and several others rode bikes around town.**

Knight: We just rode bikes because we rode bikes [laughs]. Everybody rode bikes. So the whole hallway, the porches, the sidewalks would be full of bikes. There was always a bike to be loaned, too, if somebody came into town. I didn't know how to drive. I didn't learn how to drive until a year and a half ago because it was so easy to get around.

**What made you decide to learn to drive?**

Knight: Oh, at a late age? I have a daughter and it was just easier to. My life circumstances changed a little bit and so it was a necessity.

**I guess we can start talking about the house. How did you come upon 309?**

Knight: When I first moved back from San Francisco, a bunch of my friends lived here so I would come and hang out. Eventually, I was here all the time. Then Rymodee and I started dating. We dated for a long time, so we were always here.

**What were your first impressions of the house?**

Knight: The house? I mean, these folks were like family to me. It wasn't really an impression like, "Everybody lives in a house that's crazy, that has flyers on the walls and thrift store couches." That was just the way everybody's houses looked—everybody that had roommates. So it wasn't any different.

**Did you live at 309?**

Knight: No. I stayed here a lot, but I never lived here as a roommate or a tenant.

**What went into your decision to not live here?**

Knight: I have my own house [laughs]. Yeah, I had my own house and my own space and my own stuff, and all of that. I was here every day, but I had my own space.

**Why did you become a vegan?**

Knight: I wanted to live more compassionately and feel better about decisions I was making. To feel better about the food I was eating and where it was coming from.

**Were other people in the punk community vegan?**

Knight: There were a lot, but it was a mixed bag. There wasn't anywhere to eat, so we cooked a lot and had a lot of potlucks. We always had extra food, and we fed everybody that was at the house when we cooked. So there was a handful of vegan people, but everybody ate vegan when we were cooking.

**Can you describe the kinds of food you guys would eat at these potlucks?**

Knight: Oh god. In the beginning, it was not the most balanced, healthiest diet ever. We ate a lot of potatoes and gravy, and couscous and gravy, and biscuits and, you know, we'd throw in some broccoli. Everything had gravy on it. A lot of tofu in a skillet. A lot of cast iron skillets with a lot of oil and then muffins and cakes. It was real heavy. At the beginning, we made so much heavy food. Then we lightened up, started making stuff a little lighter, which was good.

**Was there ever a rift between those who were vegan and not?**

Knight: Like a war? [Laughs]

**Well, not like a war, but any arguments over it?**

Knight: Every once in a while there'd be somebody drunk at a bar who'd bring something up that was dumb. It was basically their own insecurity.

**What was it like to be a vegan in nineties Pensacola?**

Knight: Hungry! But that's why we cooked so much. That's why we had so many potlucks. We'd have potlucks everywhere, all over town. We'd bike our food, sit around and eat because there wasn't any place. You could go to a restaurant and you could get, like, pizzas without cheese. I just thought it was terrible. They'd order a pizza without cheese, bring it back, make a vegan cheese sauce, and put it on there. It tasted bad, but in a pinch people did that. We could go to Tu-Do and get Vietnamese food, and we were there probably three or four times a week sometimes, but other than that we just did a lot of cooking and that was a big part of our community.

**How has being a vegan in Pensacola changed since you first became vegan?**

Knight: Ooooh, child [laughs]. A lot. It's changed a lot. It definitely has the uptick since it's gone mainstream and there's a lot of people more vocal about it now. Then, it was either hippie food or people just didn't care to know about it. Or they thought the only thing we ate was, you know, fried dirt, boiled water, or granola and salads. Some people would laugh when you would say the word "vegan." Now everybody knows what that word means. So, it's definitely changed. Huge. Hugely, if that's a word.

**Where did the idea for having a vegan restaurant come from?**

Knight: One of the things that we did here at 309 was the Spare Change Cafe. Since there wasn't any place to go eat, we decided to build our own little cafe. It was a suggested donation of three-to-five bucks for food. We had somebody waiting tables, somebody doing dishes, and somebody cooking, and it would rotate each time. Then we had the opportunity to make a move on the cafe across the street, where the owners were leaving, and take that over.

**Where was the Spare Change Cafe?**

Knight: Right here on the porch of 309. You'd sit on chairs or milk crates, or like I'm sitting on the stoop, and they'd bring you out a glass of water and a plate of food. It was massive portions of tofu steak and couscous, or spaghetti, or seitan ribs, with all kinds of different sides. It was really fun. It was nice being out here on the porch, people sitting on the steps inside, people sitting on the ground.

**Was it just a thing for the punks and whoever else knew about it?**

Knight: For anybody. Anybody at all. Everybody got really excited when it wasn't one of the punks. We're like, "Yes! Let me pull you up a milk crate to sit on. You have to eat in your lap because we don't really have tables."

**What was the building where End of the Line is now?**

Knight: It was Van Gogh's Coffee Haus. It was just a coffeehouse, and some of our friends worked there.

**Can you walk me through what it looked like as Van Gogh's?**

Knight: It had couches and art on the walls. It had mismatched furniture, but not mismatched like in a thrift store—new mismatched furniture and very angular tables. Tables where you run into them and it really hurt you. These weird artistic tables, but artistic in a sense that it was made to look artistic, not handmade.

**I read that it was kind of a yuppie space beforehand.**

Knight: I think that's what they wanted it to be. At that time, there weren't really any coffee shops in Pensacola. That was something that was unfamiliar to Pensacola. People would come in and ask, "Hey, can I have my coffee in one of those big mugs like they do on that show *Friends*?" That's kind of what they were going for—that whole *Friends* vibe.

**When did the space start changing?**

Knight: When our friends all worked there. Bringing in poetry readings and an open mic was the introduction to a different vibrancy, or a vibrancy at all, to that place. Then they started having shows.

**Whose idea was it to create a vegan cafe?**

Knight: We were just taking it over as a coffee shop. We didn't intend to be a restaurant in the beginning, we just wanted to keep that space in the community and not have it be some weird nightclub in the middle of the neighborhood and next to 309. We wanted to keep the open mics going, keep doing shows, and keep this nice little hangout space. Then it evolved on its own. We started realizing that we weren't paying the rent from coffee. We started making muffins and sandwiches, and it went in stages from there.

**Did you guys change the space at all or was it the same exact coffee shop, just a different name on the sign?**

Knight: Oh, it changed so many times. We pulled the carpet out and got rid of that. We painted the walls. We really didn't want it to be Van Gogh's. We kept the fish. There was a big devilfish named Lucifer, and we kept him. In the beginning we tried to do it as a collective, and there were different volunteers and different people working. We still had shows occasionally and that open mic. Eventually, it just became a full restaurant.

**Where do you guys get your food products from?**

Knight: Now it's all distributors. We have two natural foods distributors. Back then we rode our bikes everywhere and loaded it up on our trailers. We would ride our bikes with the trailers all the way out to Brownsville to pick up our tofu from My Tan, the little Vietnamese market that would order it for us. We'd ride our bikes all the way over to Bailey's Farmer's Market and load our baskets full of vegetables. We'd ride up to Albertson's and load up on orange juice and soy milk to make cappuccinos. We didn't have any distributors. We had a coffee distributor and that was it.

**Was End of the Line respected as a business within the larger Pensacola business community in the first few years?**

Knight: No way [laughs]. Not at all.

**Has it changed over time, or do you still feel there's a disconnect?**

Knight: It definitely has changed because people's diets have changed, but I think that End of the Line is always going to be its own unique little piece of Pensacola. You know, people come in, "Oh, it looks so different!" And I'm like, "Well, I just peeled the duct tape off the walls and wiped off the Sharpie, but the heart is going to always be the same."

**Do you think this relates to the idea of punk and it being counter-cultural? Do you feel that running a business conflates with the punk ideal, the punk root?**

Knight: Absolutely. I think these are really exciting times, seeing a lot of people that were in the punk community in the eighties and nineties being adult business owners now, and having a small part in how this city is moving into the future.

**Besides End of the Line, what other businesses have come out of 309 and the punk scene here?**

Knight: Lots. There's several different tattoo shops. There's sign companies. There's metal crafters. There's furniture stores. There's jewelry stores. There's more restaurants. There's bars. There's people in law. There's people in every different facet.

**There's been a mixture of reactions from people about putting punk into a museum format. What are your feelings about 309 becoming a museum?**

Knight: Honestly, when all over social media people were saying, "Let's get together and buy 309," I thought it was a terrible idea. I was like, "You guys can't all come together and buy a house. There's a lot of paperwork involved. If you're going to collectively do something, you all have to be on the same page and have a projected view." Then Scott got involved. As soon as Scott Satterwhite got involved, I knew it could happen. I knew it could be organized. I knew that it was an actual possibility and that it wasn't just a bunch of people that were sad their memories were going to get sold.

**As kind of a wrap-up question, why is 309 significant to you?**

Knight: Because of all of those memories, and the laughter—like gut-cramping, bent over, I'm going to pee my pants laughter. That kind of fun like, "We can't wait until we can do that again." And having seen all the art that's come out of here go in so many different directions. I think what makes the place special is that it has become its own punk, you know? It has become its own entity.

# Scott Satterwhite

"I had already served my time"

**To begin, what brought you to Pensacola?**

Satterwhite: I was in the Navy and I got stationed here. They let you choose—well, not really choose, but you write down the three places that you want to go, and they say they'll try their best to get you to one of those three. I chose San Diego, San Francisco, and Seattle. I got my orders and mine said Pensacola, Florida [laughs].

**Are you currently still active?**

Satterwhite: Oh, no. No, no, no. I got out of the Navy four years after I got here. I was mentally done with all that.

**You mentioned that Pensacola wasn't in your first three choices, but it seems like you've liked it enough to stay around.**

Satterwhite: I ended up liking it. When I got here, I was getting into punk. A lot of people my age were, with Nirvana and things like that. I don't want to try and grab some old school cred. It would be easy because no one would know, but it was literally Kurt Cobain that got me into punk. I'd see Kurt Cobain on *Saturday Night Live* or on MTV, and he's wearing a band T-shirt, so I'd look up that band. They were almost all small, independent bands. I'd find the band and get their records. Then I did the same thing with those other bands—I'd see the shirt they're wearing, and the bands they're talking about. I'm getting to your question in a second.

**No, you're doing great.**

Satterwhite: Here in Pensacola, there was a little record store called the Sound Box, and that's where I spent a lot of my money and a lot of time. They had all these flyers for shows that were taking place, and zines, and it was the first time I had really looked at zines. I picked up the zines and would read stories about people in the local scene, people

I didn't know. I'm looking at those zines and then looking at the flyers, and I started going to shows with my girlfriend at the time, Keisha. We went to Sluggo's just about every chance we could get. There was this one bartender who would always remember our drinks. He'd even light her cigarettes. I guess I was a little bit of an outsider, which was why I was happy he remembered those small things. It was pretty welcoming.

**What did your parents do? You mentioned your father was in the Navy as well. Is that your biological dad, or your stepdad?**

Satterwhite: Actually, both of them were in the Navy. My dad was drafted during Vietnam. He was a corpsman in the Navy, so we had that in common and not a lot else. Well, you're not drafted into the Navy, but you're drafted into the Army. When he got his draft notice he quick ran over to the Navy recruiters so he didn't have to go into the jungles of Vietnam like his brother did. His brother was MIA a few times, got letters from the government sent home and all, but he came back. Evidently that scared my dad, but he didn't realize that the field he had chosen was one that you had a good chance to go into the Marine Corps, so that actually puts you in a lot more danger. But he didn't end up going to Vietnam, and instead went to Bethesda, Maryland, to the Navy hospital there, which was where I was conceived.

**What was your mother's occupation? Was she a stay-at-home mom, or did she have a career?**

Satterwhite: She was a stay-at-home mom until my dad left. They had five kids. That's a lot. Then my dad left us and she started watching other kids for pay—about two hundred neighborhood kids, it seemed. She didn't really have any other marketable skill, and there's not a lot you can do when you have five young kids. My dad hardly ever paid child support, too. She supported us through doing that and pretty much every other social system that was around: food stamps, church communities, Reagan cheese. Whatever she could do to keep us all afloat.

**Can you tell me about some of your earliest memories of 309?**

Satterwhite: I started doing my own zine, which I still do now. Through selling them at Sluggo's and at this small independent bookstore called Subterranean Books, I was able to meet a lot of people in the scene. Eventually I started selling their zines too, including the one by the bartender I was telling you about, Skott Cowgill. But I had never been to 309 yet, and it was the place where the coolest people in the Pensacola punk scene lived. The people that owned Sluggo's lived here. The people that played in Woodenhorse lived here. The people in This Bike is a Pipe Bomb lived here.

The first time I actually went to the house was when Sarah Hill invited me to a show here. I'd known Sarah from Subterranean Books, and we became pretty good friends. She was in the hardcore scene locally, and she went to shows all the time. She would talk me into going to tons of shows, probably because I had a car. She told me there was a show taking place over at 309, it was the band Rainer Maria. I was excited because Rainer Maria was pretty big, but they were friends with Skott Cowgill and I guess he invited them to play. They set up in the living room and played a show. So my first memory is coming into that show, giving a small donation at the door, and then I hung out watching the band from the stairs. I'm actually looking at those stairs right now.

**Oh, wow! You're currently at the house?**

Satterwhite: Yeah, I'm at 309 right now.

**Oh, very cool. And did you move into the house after that, or was—**

Satterwhite: Yeah, I moved in not long after. I actually lived right next door first. I was distributing Rex's zine, so we got to talking and he said he had a place next door to 309, and it was only two hundred dollars. He was looking for roommates. I thought, "Great! I can live next to 309 and be closer to the scene going on there." We split the two hundred between three people, so sixty-six a month for me. Remember, I had just gotten out of the Navy. I got a severance check, so I paid three or four months in advance.

That was my first introduction to 309 as a culture instead of just a house. 311 was fairly small, but I had a lot of friends who were living in 309. Two people I became close with were Shari and Ada. They were dating and sharing a room in the back of 309, and they would come over to 311 all the time. Eventually a room opened up over at 309. Shari and Ada liked me enough and thought I'd be a nice fit in the house. As soon as I could, I moved next door.

I was a little sad to leave 311, but the house was a total wreck. Not to say 309 was by any means nice and clean, but at 311 everything was falling apart. You couldn't sit on the toilet and lean too far over or the whole toilet would fall through the floor. As soon as you tried to sit down on the toilet, it moved a little to the right. Then you could see through the floor to the ground underneath it. It was a little precarious every time you went to the bathroom. And Rex had a dog, and the dog had fleas. He either couldn't afford medicine or didn't care about the fleas. Whatever it was, the house was covered in fleas. He had read that pennyroyal could get rid of fleas, and maybe it did, but not the way he used it. The house was covered in all of these little seeds from the pennyroyal.

The house was dirty as hell. It was hot. It was so, so hot. The house was falling apart, everything's dirty, and then one of my roommates—who I loved dearly—was this total crazy drunk maniac, and she would come home all wasted and screaming at the top of her lungs. "Scotty Potty, wake up!" It was just a little more chaotic than I could handle. So when Shari and Ada told me there was a room opening at 309, I quickly said yes. I apologized to my friends for abandoning them, but I abandoned them and packed up my things and moved next door. I lived at 309 from then on, from 1999 until the fall of 2007.

**Can you describe what the house looked like then? Was it more of a shared environment or were there specific rooms for the people living there?**

Satterwhite: It depends on what room you lived in. If somebody was moving into the house, they wouldn't usually get one of the high-end rooms. Not when you first moved in. So I had one of the small rooms when I first moved in. It was a cute little place that had a bed for a little while, until the person who owned the bed asked for it back. Then it was just a mattress.

I had a window. I could look out, open up the window. It was pretty nice. Climb out and sit outside. The rent was really cheap, too. It was about as cheap as 311, maybe a little more. I wasn't working at that time, and was into the politicized form of anti-work culture. I just did not want to work a regular job anymore and participate in the system. I had already served my time. This was a great transition from the military—living in the house with multiple roommates, kind of like a halfway house. One I never moved out of.

I sold plasma over at the plasma center, and that was easily enough to live off. I also reviewed CDs for my zine, so the record companies would send CDs in the mail. Most of them sucked. I'd just give them a bad review and then ride over to the record store and sell them. Four bucks a pop. At that time, they were almost a form of currency.

It wasn't that difficult to survive, which I know sounds crazy. I went from being an aerospace physiology technician to selling plasma and CDs and living with half a dozen roommates in this crazy house. But it was the first time I'd ever felt like I was in a really tight family.

But back to your question about the rooms, I'll give you another scenario: when I moved into a bigger room downstairs, one of the people who lived there before had built this elaborate loft system. With that loft, it was almost like being a kid. You had this giant bunk bed. Eventually I had some friends who needed a place to stay. Honestly, I can't remember if they needed a place to stay or if they just wanted to stay with me, but they ended up sleeping below my bed. Samantha Dorsett lived under my bed for about six months, then Ada lived there for a bit and she shared the space under the loft.

Just because you have all these different people living with you, sleeping under the bed, in the bed sometimes, people assumed everybody was sleeping around, or that everybody was doing drugs. But at least in my experience, it wasn't like that.

**Could you tell me what was your best day spent at the house?**

Satterwhite: You said my best day?

**Yes, sir.**

Satterwhite: Hmm. Let me see. I can actually think of a bunch that were, when I look back on them, some of the best days of my life. It could be either really getting to meet and know Aaron Cometbus, sitting on the front porch. It could be when Lauren Anzaldo came knocking on my door. One night after a show, years later, we became boyfriend and girlfriend. Looking back, those were great days. But I would say probably the best day would be when my daughter was born. It was on July 20th, 2005. She spent her first night in the house. We actually built a room for her, and it was going to be her nursery, but she never slept in it. She'd cry so much. Every time we'd put her in the crib, she'd just cry and cry, so we'd bring her back into the room to be with us. I think that was the point of her crying, though. She wanted us. That first day was the best day in the house for me. Nine months after having made a baby, now the baby's in the house.

That was nice. A year after Hurricane Ivan, too. Hurricane Ivan, now that would be one of the worst days, when the city got destroyed. The back of the house got ripped off. That was a depressing experience, so having a baby after that was special. In literature, whenever there's a baby born you look at it as a symbolic moment, a kind of rebirth, resurrection, something new that comes along that changes the world. Babies do that. So Lauren being pregnant in the house was pretty wild because right before Maddy was born we had probably the most roommates we ever had in the house. That might've been because of the disruption from the hurricane, but we had about ten roommates living here. Ten roommates and four dogs and it was just crazy.

Sarah Hill was living here, and her friend Savannah. They were on fire all the time. Sarah was famous, or infamous, for getting kicked out or banned from every bar in town. She fought every sexist asshole she could, literally fought them. There was this one guy she didn't like because he was always making sexist comments. One of her friends was with her at the bar and he goes, "What would you do if that guy was sitting right next to you?"

She said, "What would I do? I'd punch him in the face!"

"Well, look to your left," and then she saw him. There he was, and she punched him in the face [laughs].

She was like a can of gasoline looking for a match. She was a better literary character than she was a roommate, at that time at least. I still have very fond memories of Sarah, and still think the world of her, but it was a wild time. With Lauren pregnant, that exacerbated any tensions. I remember one time when Lauren was approaching eight or nine months. Sarah was yelling at people as they were passing by on the street, and hanging out and partying until 3:00 or 4:00 in the morning. Lauren was like, "God! Please go down there and tell them to shut up, I need to sleep."

We had this other family living here too. They probably had the first kid in the house. It was a mom, her boyfriend, and two kids all living in one room. Having the two kids there actually helped us. Lauren and I learned how to deal with kids, to play with them, talk to them, talk at their level. This was just something I hadn't done before. Having some kids around helped. It was nice and it helped for when Maddy was born.

**Why did you leave—**

Satterwhite: As I'm saying that, I'm thinking about a bunch of other good days too.

**Oh, I'm sure. All of it starts to flood back when you start speaking on it. Can you tell me why you eventually left the house?**

Satterwhite: When Maddy was born, I realized I needed to do some kind of meaningful work. By that time I wasn't selling my blood so much, I was working at the End of the Line—in fact, I was one of the founders. But it was a collective, and because it was a collective, all the money we were making was basically going back into the cafe. It wasn't until just a few months before Maddy was born that we even started paying ourselves, and we paid ourselves minimum wage for wait staff—three dollars an hour plus tips. And we hardly got any tips.

That was okay when I didn't have a kid. But when we had a kid, that changed some things. In our early years of parenting, when Maddy was little, there were enough social services around to get by. Also, we had a friend who was a produce guy at this grocery store over in Gulf Breeze, and he'd arranged this elaborate pickup system for us to get the produce they were throwing away. It was around fourteen or fifteen boxes—banana boxes, which are really large. We'd send somebody over there Saturday at 1:00 and they'd do the food pickup, then bring it back to 309 to sort. There's no way we could eat it all, so we divided it up between the four or five other punkhouses that were around here. There was 311, they got a box. The house with all these Dominican punks from the band La Armada, they got a box. Pretty much anybody who was in our circle got this giant box of produce.

Even people outside of our circle, like the old lady at 313, Miss Katie. She was nice, but funny. We'd come in bringing the box and she'd be like, "I can't eat all this, this is too much." The woman around the corner from 309, Miss Cassandra, her family got a few boxes of food. She even returned the favor when Maddy was born and bought us a bunch of baby clothes. It's pretty amazing seeing the food boxes feeding all these people, all from one dumpster. Everyone knew where the food was coming from, too—and the food was perfectly fine. Once we sorted out the handful of rotten apples or whatever, it was all perfectly fine food. Basically, free healthy produce for years.

That was how we were living for Maddy's first two years at 309. I worked at the cafe and Lauren worked for one of the daycares. Both of us combined made below minimum wage, definitely below the poverty level. We made so little that we didn't have to report taxes because there was nothing to report, but it was enough for us to live at 309, so it didn't really matter. What the social services didn't provide, our community did. We were totally set and taken care of, but just without a lot of spending money. We didn't really need it either, because our friends were entertaining enough. We booked a lot of the shows, so we were basically setting up our own entertainment system. Movie nights at the cafe. Themed dinners. Even circuses, real circuses. We'd set up our own food distribution system. And we had driven the rent down to where I'd never once paid more than 125 dollars a month for my share of rent and utilities.

So we had a pretty ideal situation. But Lauren, who'd been to college, was smart enough to realize that this wouldn't always be the case. While what we had was amazing, it was always on pretty shaky ground. All you need is a natural disaster to throw all the stuff off, and then everybody's livelihoods are shattered. Or if the landlord decides to sell the house, we're out on the street and we've got to pay regular rent. Or if somebody gets a terrible disease, like multiple sclerosis, and that person is in charge of the food distribution, which is exactly what happened to our friend who worked over at the grocery store. Steve Winfrey ended up getting MS and couldn't work proper hours anymore. So that ended the food pickup.

All those things were on kind of shaky grounds to begin with, but when they were working, they were great. That's how we were living, but like I said, Lauren was smart enough to realize that we would probably need something else.

**Are you associated with the 309 Museum?**

Satterwhite: Yeah, I'm one of the founders. Me and Terry Johnson—we're the founders. Terry's really the founder of the project, even though she stepped back when she moved to Chattanooga. She came up to me one day at Sluggo's, "Scotty Potty, I've got this crazy idea." Four years later, I'm living in the house again.

**They call you Scotty, what was it, sorry?**

Satterwhite: Scotty Potty. Like a toilet.

**Okay. I just wanted to make sure for spelling reasons. Very nice.**

Satterwhite: Yeah. They called me that because when I first moved in,

Skott Cowgill also lived here. One time my mom called on the phone and Rymodee answered. My mom calls and says, "I'm looking to speak to Scott, is he available?"

Rymodee said, "No, he's not here right now. May I ask who's calling?"

"This is his mom."

Then Rymo got mad. He said, "Is this some kind of sick joke? His mom's dead!"

My mom freaked out. "What? He told you that I'm dead?"

And then Rymo said, "Uh, oh. Wait a minute, do you mean Scott Satterwhite or Skott Cowgill?"

**Oh my gosh.**

Satterwhite: My roommates realized they would need some other way to refer to me. Which is kind of funny because even though I was twenty-six or twenty-seven years old, here I was given the same nickname I had in kindergarten.

**So, why is 309 significant to you?**

Satterwhite: One aspect is the people living in the house who went on to create a number of businesses in Pensacola that are still active. End of the Line Cafe started here. Another is Hula Moon Tattoos. That business started in 2000 and is still around to this day. The Prison Book Project started here in 2000 also. The Prison Book Project started in the room I'm sitting in right now—the front room of 309. We had this anarchist collective, an infoshop[1] called CORE, and when it folded we had a very large lending library. We didn't know what to do with all of the books, so Shari and Ada got in touch with their friend in Asheville who had a prison book program. They got a lot of letters from Florida, so she suggested we start something similar here, and we had enough books to do it.

That was the birth of the Prison Book Project, which had its twentieth birthday this January. We even got a proclamation from the mayor for that. The mayor proclaimed January 16th Open Books Prison Book Project Day. Open Books is the bookstore that came out of the Prison Book Project. That started in 2007, about the same time I was moving out of 309.

---

1   An activist center, reading room, and space for meetings and events.

So that's at least three successful and pretty influential businesses. And then, on the national level, the house has been well known within all sorts of different scenes. It was listed in the *Crew Change Guide,* which is an underground, secret book for trainhoppers. 309 was listed in there, saying if you're in trouble on the train, there's nice people in this house and they'll treat you well. Within the punk scene, this house is where This Bike is a Pipe Bomb had its first practices. They went on to become very significant in the punk scene, in particular with bands like Against Me! who were influenced by them in a lot of ways. Also, there's this photography book that came out, *Punk House: Interiors in Anarchy.* That book has an entire chapter on 309. There are numerous pictures of people that were in the house, and of the house itself.

Besides that would be some of the more influential people that have lived here. Cindy Crabb, for instance. She wrote the zine *Doris,* and that was pretty influential. Before *Doris,* there weren't a lot of people doing really personal articles in zines, a lot of deep memoir-type work. Then Aaron Cometbus, who's by far the most influential zine writer in the country. He was a big part of this house even when he was living next door, since the buildings are so closely connected.

Probably the most culturally significant person to live here, next to Aaron and Cindy, is Mike Brodie. He would jump on freight trains, because the trains ride right in front of the house. He took his Polaroid camera and started taking pictures. He just had a really great eye, no professional training. He wasn't looking for any big attention, but the right people found these pictures and thought they were important. Luckily, he had the right people looking after him. I could see somebody like him—like most of us—getting screwed over in that kind of world, but he ended up getting a lot of fame out of these works. He has, I think, three coffee table books, and a lot of those pictures feature us. My daughter, she was in *Time* magazine because of Mike Brodie. Mike was living with us in the house at the time, and he came upstairs to see the baby. He was just like, "Oh my god, she's so cute. Can I take a picture?" It's a pretty unique honor. Maddy's laying on our bed in our bedroom, and it's just a gorgeous picture.

I could go on and on. There were so many inspiring artists and musicians who were part of the house—people like Adee Roberson, Kent Stanton, and Dave Dondero. So 309 plays a pretty big role, more so than probably any other punkhouse, definitely in the South. This area is not known for the little hotbeds of radical subcultures and countercultures, but they are totally here. What makes 309 different is that it's a really longstanding site. 309 is the oldest continuously inhabited punkhouse in all of the South, and now punks own it. It's crazy to think about. If you would've told me in 1999, when I first got to the house, that any of this stuff would have happened I'd be shocked beyond belief.

**I think we're getting to the point where we're going to wrap up. Is there anything you'd like to discuss further?**

Satterwhite: Mmm. Here's something. I'll tell you one little story. It's a short one, don't worry. When I turned thirty, Aaron and Paula wanted to do a little party for me. I was booking punk shows over at the cafe, but I had no intentions of doing a show on my birthday. I wanted to sit around and read a book or do something quiet. Turning thirty is a milestone, for whatever reason. It's not just another birthday, but one of those when you get a zero at the end. They become a big deal—especially thirty—so I was feeling weird about the whole thing. I didn't want to do a show that night, but there was a band that sounded interesting. Like a good radical, I should mention that I was fascinated with Soviet history, going back from when I was in the military. Aaron was also fascinated with Soviet history, so we'd talk about it a lot. This band called Communist Conspiracy Rhythm wanted to do a show. I thought, "Hmm, that's interesting. They want to play on my birthday." Well, I get an email a few days later, "Hey, I'm in this band called Stalin's War" [laughs]. Stalin's War wanted to play at the cafe on the same day. So I thought, "Yeah, this will be fun."

I thought we'd have a theme party. From there Aaron and Paula took over and I just handled the show part. Aaron made this giant mural behind the stage. For a backdrop, the bands would have this big picture of Fidel Castro and Nikita Khrushchev. The two of them were hugging each other in this bear hug, maybe from the United Nations, either right before or right after the Cuban missile crisis. He made this mural out of photographs, as big as the wall. Then they cut up all the red sheets from the house and made these red flags, and draped them all the way up and down the street. Every telephone pole for a half-mile radius had these red flags, just as if Nikita Khrushchev was coming to the cafe. So they hung up all these red flags down the streets to greet the bands.

Then the big thing they did, they painted the entire sidewalk red, from 309 to 311. So the sidewalk is painted red, red flags are all up and down the streets, and Nikita Khrushchev and Fidel Castro are hanging up on this mural in the cafe. The cafe is covered in all these red flags. Covered in communism. These two bands—Communist Conspiracy and Stalin's War—get to the cafe and don't even mention it. The funniest thing, or saddest, was that neither of the bands said anything about the stuff. Apparently both bands, like most bands, had kind of dumb names that they thought were fun. Neither of them were communist or anything like that. We asked them, "Are you Stalinists?"

They were like, "No, why would you think that?"

"Well, your name is Stalin's War."

I wonder, did they think Pensacola was normally like Moscow in 1960 or something? They didn't even notice any of the stuff, and just thought it was perfectly normal that this little cafe in the Deep South had this giant mural of Castro and Khrushchev, and red flags are draping the entire city. They played. I don't remember either band being terribly interesting. They do their thing, they leave, and then Aaron says at the end of the night, "I've got one more birthday present to show you." And that's when they unveiled the red sidewalk. I just thought it was the sweetest thing.

Afterwards we all got drunk and actually had some fun seeing the old Pensacola punk band Maggot Sandwich practice for a reunion show. They were just practicing, but ended up playing for us, so it was another nice birthday present. And somebody made me a key lime pie, which is a birthday tradition with me ever since I moved to Florida.

Well, a couple days later the landlord comes knocking on the door and says, "Hey, man, I think it looks really cool. I think it's awesome that you guys did this, but now the city's getting on my ass because you painted the sidewalk red." [Laughs]

But the funny thing was that he wanted to clean it up, not us. "Yeah, don't worry. I'm going to take care of it. I'll fix it. I'll do it, I just wanted to let you know." He was like, "I'm sorry, if it was up to me, we could paint the whole city red, but we can't leave this here."

So he takes off all the red paint. The only thing he left was a little heart in front of the house. After all of those birthday things, he leaves a red heart in front of the house on the sidewalk. When Aaron came walking up the street, I showed him the heart. It was one of the sweetest things I had ever seen. Then Aaron said, "Come on Scotty, let's go get a cup of coffee."

Suckcesspool gameboard.

*Right*: Skott Cowgill on 309 porch.

*Below*: Terry Johnson. Photo by Scott Satterwhite.

*Left*: Shari Rother, Rymodee, and Skott Cowgill as Spare Change Cafe staff.

*Below*: Rymodee. Photo by Martin Werneth.

Big Dave and Gabe Smith help get the message out. Photo by Ben Mistak.

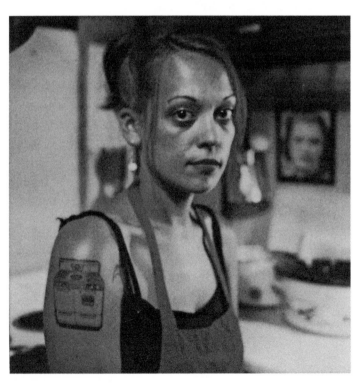

Jen Knight.
Photo by Mike
Brodie.

Rex Ray and Rebecca Redbait at Van Gogh's. Photo by Rex Ray.

Scott Satterwhite at 309. Photo by Abby Banks.

Aaron Cometbus at 311, Pensacola, Florida, 4-16-2003. Copyright 2003 Cynthia Connolly.

Steve Winfrey at 309 with his daughters Tessa and Caitlyn. Photo by Scott Satterwhite.

*Above*: Crystal Tremer and Scott Satterwhite.

*Left*: 311 Kitchen. Photo by Arwen Curry.

Aaron Cometbus at Subterranean Books, Pensacola, Florida, 1-27-2003. Copyright 2003 Cynthia Connolly.

Samantha Dorsett and Ada Johnson in front of Subterranean Books. Photo by Scott Satterwhite.

Kent Stanton and Gloria Diaz. Photo by Scott Satterwhite.

Lauren Anzaldo and Adee Roberson. Photo by Scott Satterwhite.

*Right*: Lauren Anzaldo.
Photo by Mike Brodie.

*Below*: Madailein
Anzaldo-Satterwhite.
Photo by Mike Brodie.

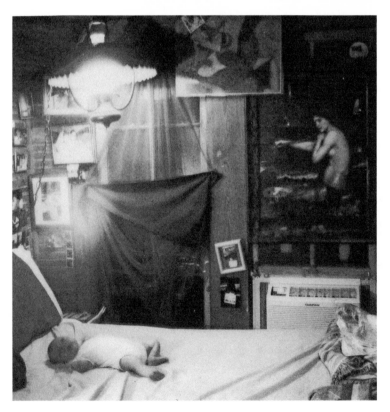

*Left*: Donald Yeo. Photo by Mike Brodie.

*Below*: Eliza Espy and Valerie George. Photo by Scott Satterwhite.

Barrett Williamson. Photo by Scott Satterwhite.

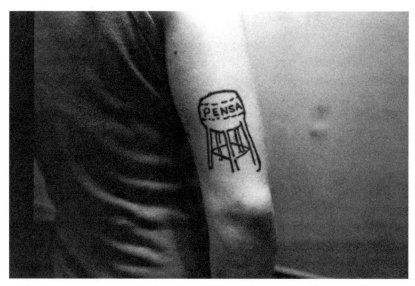

Pensacola Tattoo #1, 6-19-2003. Copyright 2003 Cynthia Connolly.

309 after Hurricane Ivan. Photo by Abby Banks.

Pensacola Tattoo #4, 6-19-2003. Copyright 2003 Cynthia Connolly.

# Aaron Cometbus

"You become part of the history"

**I'm going to first ask a couple background questions. What is your full name?**

Cometbus: I don't actually go by Aaron Cometbus, but it's my literary identity, so it makes sense to use it for this.

**Do you mind saying how you came up with the pseudonym Cometbus?**

Cometbus: Oh, sure. I've been doing the fanzine for going on forty years. In the early days it changed names every issue, and there would be contests to name it. One of the contest winners was "Ride the Wohl Whip Cometbus." The guy now known as Neil Hamburger, the comedian, came up with that, and it became the fanzine's steady name. And in my circles, if you do something long enough, you unfortunately take on the name of whatever it is you do.

**Awesome. Where were you born?**

Cometbus: I was born in Berkeley, California.

**Did you grow up there as well?**

Cometbus: I did. I grew up there and had never been further than Sacramento, which is about one hundred miles, until I left on tour with my first band in 1988. A week and a half into the two-and-a-half month tour the band imploded, and it imploded in Pensacola. So by the time I finally left home I did not get very far, and I ended up on the corner of Palafox and Cervantes, not far from what became 309.

**So when the band imploded and got dropped off in Pensacola, how long did it take you to realize you wanted to stay there?**

Cometbus: Twenty years [laughs]. In fact, the joke was on me, because the people who later became central figures at 309 were the ones that caught us in our fall—who made us feel like it was a natural occurrence to have your band break up and get dropped off with no vehicle or equipment, and only two members left. So I felt a kinship for Pensacola right away, but there was no idea in the slightest that I would want to live there.

**Did you play a show in Pensacola when you first got there, or did you ever get to play that show?**

Cometbus: Yes, we played. We got dropped off and we called the promoter—the promoter was Skott Cowgill—and he said, "Sure, I know how it is. You can meet me at my job at the Christian surf shop. Things don't always work out how you expected them to." His job being a case in point. Basically, everyone who was part of the Pensacola punk scene was endeared to us because of the ridiculousness of our situation, so they came up onstage and jumped alongside us to add stage presence, and they brought us into their homes. I also met Rymodee and Terry. We played at her early club one of the next nights because we were stranded. It began a long-time relationship with Pensacola.

**So with Skott being the promoter, you said the name of the club you played the first night was "Christian Surf Shop"?**

Cometbus: No, no, no. Never mind that. Parts of his life were just like the punch line to a joke. So me calling to say that my band had arrived, but we had arrived without any equipment or vehicle, was similar to his life at the moment. It resonated. The club was called the Mix and it was short-lived—one of many short-lived late eighties punk clubs.

**The show you played the second night, what club was that?**

Cometbus: I don't know if it was the second night. Not only did we not have a vehicle, but we didn't know how to drive. Eventually we got a ride to Tallahassee, but I think it might have taken a week. So sometime during that week, Terry let us jump on a bill at—it was before Sluggo's and it was called—oh, Victor Hugo's. It was called Victor Hugo's.

**Because you were a touring band, what were the differences between the punk scene of Pensacola and some of the scenes you had previously been in?**

Cometbus: It's not that Pensacola really had anything going for it. It didn't have resources or well-known bands. But there was a scrappy enthusiasm. People cared. When we played Tallahassee, no one cared.

Pensacola was certainly not the most happening place in the country—it was not special in that way. But it was special in a down-home, shortest-straw-picked kind of way.

**You said that people from the 309 house helped you out. Did you start staying at 309 almost immediately after being dropped off?**

Cometbus: That came much later. Skott ended up living there many years later. Rymodee ended up living there many years later. It's a little unclear to me when it began, but I visited Pensacola almost every year and it didn't figure into the narrative of people I knew until much later on.

**Oh, I see.**

Cometbus: There was a funny history of different—I don't want to say this in a bad way, but of failures. There was the Rat House, there was a Rat House II, there was a Rat House III. There was a long history of these attempts to have a group house that had an identity and a name. I think that had been given up on, and people just had their little apartments. That part of the early Pensacola punk idealism had pretty much passed. Everyone had moved on to a different part of their lives, and then it came back together unexpectedly.

**So you weren't necessarily living in Pensacola from '88. You were still touring?**

Cometbus: No, I didn't move there until 1999. I had no intention to live there, but I would come through every year with a different band and play a show and see the same people. It wasn't like this growing thing that was amazing, it was this burst of energy that quickly got sad and dead and tragic. Skott had a terrible house fire. People were getting strung out and disappearing. It all got fractured. People were getting married and joining the military, and it was as if it had all finished. What was surprising about 309 was that it was this same family of people that then kind of regrouped.

I had been living in Asheville. Me and my girlfriend at the time, Cindy Crabb, were trying to make a scene. We built a club, and we both did fanzines, and we were doing all sorts of things in this other Southern city, but it was not going that great. We were expending a huge amount of energy to make things happen, yet the feeling wasn't that good. When we came to visit Pensacola, it was a bit of a shock because there were less people and less resources, but we'd go to 309 and they had the Spare Change Cafe, where they would make a four-course vegan meal—pay whatever you want, open to the public—three, four days a week. It was outrageous.

We were pretty idealistic, but the idealism wasn't doing anything for us where we were. Then we'd come to Pensacola where the food was delicious, and see people working hard and being excited and not cynical. We'd been trying to make a scene happen almost against people's will, and in Pensacola it was the opposite: everyone was really receptive. What's more, it may be a Navy city, but we walked down the street and no one yelled at us. In Asheville, this supposedly liberal enclave, you had to wear headphones because of how many people would yell "faggot" at you, or catcall women. It was super oppressive.

So it was funny to be in Pensacola and look around. "Okay, it seems like a tolerant place without much happening. But there's this little scene that's really enthusiastic and diehard, and the city is at least tolerant. This is like heaven."

**Do you think the Navy being in Pensacola maybe helped the culture grow? What do you think was helping this subculture gain momentum?**

Cometbus: Sometimes you just need a couple of people to look up to, and everyone else kind of imitates them. People were imitating Rymodee, Skott Cowgill and Terry, all who had good attitudes and were funny. The military certainly played a part because a lot of the people who lived at 309 were ex-military. I didn't understand that at first, but it meant that they had lived with peer pressure and people telling them what to do. They came out of it like, "I will never take an order from anyone. I will never care what anyone thinks so long as I am being true to, not just my own values, but to the values of the group that *I* choose." Veterans often talk about a fondness for that feeling of unit pride. I think the 309 folks wanted that too, but they wanted to choose their own unit. It was the same with family. Sure, you want a family, but you want a chosen family.

**Would you have called it a punkhouse, by definition?**

Cometbus: That's what it was, but it's not like we ever said that word. I don't want to fight against other people's preconceptions too much, but it's interesting what a punkhouse means to the people involved compared to what it might indicate to an outsider. To me, it mostly meant a heightened sense of creative involvement, but also creative output—almost an exaggerated sense, where every single person did a fanzine and every room had something going on. There was even a typewriter in the bathroom that people would use while on the toilet, and a fanzine that came from that.

**You mentioned moving there because in Asheville you were trying to start creative projects. What type of projects were you able to complete or even just begin at 309?**

Cometbus: The thing I'm good at is finishing things, so there's nothing I've ever begun and didn't finish. I think that was actually an important part of 309: there were a lot of ridiculous ideas, but they weren't just "someday" ideas. In a way, this is where I fit in because I'm a little more caffeinated and a little more of a driver type. I'm pushy, and I think it worked well there, at least initially. They had the ideas and they had the energy, but it was a good combination, like me and Scotty is a good combination, because I'm a little more point-by-point seeing things through.

It's absurd how many things happened there. An important point, though, is that I lived at 309 very briefly. I lived at 311, which is next door, for years. 311 is a much smaller house and it wasn't a group house, it was mostly just me. So most of what I'm speaking of is not actually about living at 309, per se. Okay, you ready for the list of stuff?

**Yes.**

Cometbus: Well, there's just normal house things like I'm gardening in back of 311, everyone is cooking all the time, and on the stove is also a big pot of wheat paste because we're wheat pasting the city constantly—first with our artwork and stencils, then later with protest literature and anti-war flyers. There's the slow boil of house things, but also all the ways we engaged, or tried to engage, with the rest of the city. We can get into Subterranean Books separately, but that was a bookstore Scotty was involved in, and I became involved in, and I started a monthly calendar based out of the store. It was about events around town and also about history. There'd be a lot of historical data, a lot of international holidays. Me and Scotty and other people would ride around distributing them and gathering info. He would go to Movement For Change.[1] I would go to Temple Beth-El. Samantha Dorsett would go to the Gulf Pride shop. There'd be reports about karaoke at

---

1  A local civil rights organization fighting for racial justice.

Emerald City or concerts at Seville Square, but also all the stuff we were trying to make happen.

I think that our two houses were responsible for probably fifty percent of the vandalism and artwork in downtown Pensacola, which was crazy. It looked like a swarm of people had been painting things and defacing the Andrew Jackson statue day and night, like a thousand people. It was really just this handful of people. This may sound facetious, but it was a kind of civic pride. It wasn't like breaking windows, it was trying to make the city more alive, more colorful. Although I think we were responsible for fifty percent of the vandalism, we were responsible for something like ninety-five percent of the city's actual life at the time, at least downtown. We had the bookstore. There was a club called Room 1026 some of us were connected with. We became more and more involved in Van Gogh's, which became the End of the Line. There was the Handlebar, which was run by some of the other punks I met when I first got dropped off in town, who were like extended family of 309. We also had the CORE house, which was an attempt at a community center that sometimes had shows.

So there were all these things we were involved in, and we would make rounds further and further out, trying to network. Eventually the weekly paper started printing our Subterranean Calendars. They actually started doing it without permission, which was great. They got a lot of response from troops at the base because they were from all over the world, and this was the only thing in Pensacola that reflected their experience—which talked about different holidays and different cultures and trying to integrate them and show that Pensacola was diverse. Diverse not just culturally and racially but also in opinions and beliefs—certainly more diverse than the daily paper was trying to present and the Chamber of Commerce was trying to present.

And if you'll allow me, I will continue with the list. How are you feeling about this so far?

**Yeah, I would love to keep hearing the list.**

Cometbus: Okay. So there's a bank right on Palafox, it's called the G&L Bank—Gay and Lesbian bank. Well, I'm from San Francisco and there's no gay and lesbian bank. So something was happening in Pensacola that people didn't even realize was special and unique. There's the Native American Center. There's the mosque. We were trying to tie it all together a little. Meanwhile, what else was happening? Well, we had

Steve's food pickup and distribution. We did the board game, which is called Suckcesspool. We had the Vietnamese class, and were learning Vietnamese at the bookstore. We were having these lecture dinners, like historical lectures once a month or so. There was Flat Broke Folk, which was an open mic night at Van Gogh's but also a whole group of acoustic singers and songwriters.

These are all things that 309 wasn't necessarily the center of, but just to give an example of what was happening at the time, and that 309 wasn't an island, because there was all this different interesting stuff that overlapped. We had "anarchist soccer" every Sunday, it was actually huge. A lot of people would come. There was a huge poetry scene, there were a lot of people painting. There were the surfers and skaters who were also, many of them, poets and writers, like Dan Pretto, who lived in the neighborhood. So there's all that stuff and, not to mention, of course, the bands and shows. There's a lot going on. That's even before the protests, which became three times a week and the flyering for them was every night.

**Just to confirm, you said a lot of these activities were happening between you at 311 and the people at 309. How long did you actually live at 309?**

Cometbus: I only lived at 309 a few months. I wouldn't even say it was between me and 309. I would just say it was at 309, and I lived next door. I contributed to it, but my two-room house was just sort of a doghouse for 309. So I would keep the focus there and with the people there. Also Shari who lived at 309 put out compilation tapes of that folk scene and helped articulate it as a scene by calling it Flat Broke Folk. Rymodee would play acoustic, Skott painted, and Scotty was also a poet. So you could see all these young people coming up in Pensacola who were all painting, they were all poets, and they were all singer-songwriters. It seemed completely normal to them to have all of those artistic scenes as one thing that was part of, or adjacent to, punk.

**I am actually familiar with the game that you're talking about. I used to own it.**

Cometbus: I heard. I heard you had one. That's awesome. It was ridiculous. It was a very elaborate game about Pensacola's punk history, which came with a compilation tape, and we sold it for a dollar. My slogan for the Subterranean Calendars was "Fill in the blanks," which is not the slogan I would use now, but the idea was that we should just be frantic, making and creating this culture, and then see what grew out of it.

What happened was that a lot of people moved to Pensacola just out of the fact that there was so much happening, which was funny. We would have an over-thirty skate run every week. We would jog at 11:00 every night, leaving 309 and running all along the waterfront. Everyone was into creative stuff, but also trying to be healthy.

**Because you were busy with all these projects—all the games and the calendars and flyering—did you have a nine-to-five-type job that supported this? Or were you able to support yourself just through these other ventures?**

Cometbus: Right. That's a good question. Well, besides everything else, I do a fanzine. It's not just a hobby, it's a full-time job that makes a small—very small—income. And one of the reasons I lived in Pensacola was the rent. When I lived at 309, I would visit 311. This guy named Rex lived there, and his rent was two hundred dollars. His landlord used to play bass for Ike and Tina Turner, and was a pretty nice guy.[2] I told Rex, "If you ever give this up, call me." I'd actually left Pensacola and was living in New York when he called.

He said, "I'm giving it up."

I was like, "Oh, great, I'll take it. When are you giving it up?"

He's like, "Today." [Laughs]

I was in the middle of some other life, but I just really wanted it. The magazine was not enough to support me in New York. It's not enough to support me anywhere but Pensacola. I'd also played music for years and I made a small amount of royalties from that. So I made enough from the bands and the magazine to pay two hundred dollars a month, which was great because the bookstore did not pay. It was me and Scotty working for free. He worked two days a week. I worked there one day a week.

**Were there any challenges to living next door to 309, or was that really convenient?**

Cometbus: It was just natural. I mean, there were no challenges. Oh, there actually were challenges. Everyone would be on the porch in nice weather, and I'm more of a private person. You walk out your door and everyone knows your business.

---

2  Funk/Country musician "Professor" Earl Lett.

Also, I was excited at first because people were so enthusiastic. Later I realized they were enthusiastic about anything. People would just jump on whatever was happening. Eventually these boat guys showed up in town and everyone started building boats. It's totally inconvenient to live next to 309 when people are hammering away and dragging all this rough lumber to the porch to start working on their boats, which of course never reached completion.

But that's about it. Everything else was like a dream come true. And I have to say, it wasn't like we were being martyrs by taking on all this stuff. It was a natural creative renaissance and a bit of a crush between all the different people, where everyone wanted to contribute and impress each other. And I was not expecting, at that time in my life, to have a scene. I did not move there for a scene. I moved there just for a cheap place to live, really, and quiet. But what happened was that we ended up with the scene that we wished we'd had, or that we longed for, that we thought would never happen again.

The icing on the cake was that, besides all this other stuff, me and Scotty had started a press. It was called Sub City and its purpose was to put out literature from around the world. It was mostly fiction, but some of it was political, and arguably just putting out fiction from around the world has a political subtext. The logo for our press was the water tower that Scotty drew, and me and Scotty got water tower tattoos to celebrate. It was a reference to a song by This Bike is a Pipe Bomb, which had turned into sort of a sentimental rallying cry for our scene.

Well, I think you know the story. There's something like fifty people now that have these water tower tattoos. Each one is unique and each one has its own flourish. But I'd already had a youth, and I'd already had crews of like-minded people. The last thing I expected when I moved to Pensacola was that I would be part of a youth gang with matching tattoos, and that we would have this whole brotherhood and sisterhood that was that tight and that rad.

**Do you remember who tattooed you, or was it one person tattooing everybody in the crew?**

Cometbus: Well, but here's the thing: the "crew" idea is loose and it would be easy to misunderstand this as a single, unified group. It *is* a group of people, but I don't know most of the people who got the water tower tattoo. I don't know most of the people who lived in 309. That's what's special about it. I have something in common with people I've never met, but they lived in the same room as me, different years. They probably lived there ten times longer.

That's how I felt about Pensacola, and in a way, how I feel about punk: it's something that when you take it on, you become part of the history. The history becomes your own a little bit, and you can uphold it, though you don't have to be held back by it. For me, one of the coolest things about 309 is that there's all these people that are part of it. They might have come around later, they might have come around earlier. Maybe they're part of this whole water tower thing, but they're not people I know personally. I have no idea who tattooed most of them and we didn't all go together. It wasn't like the Rats, Skott Cowgill's earlier group of young punks. It wasn't anything like that. It was really just me and Scotty and then, you know, Crystal Tremer was like, "You guys didn't ask me if I wanted to get one."

"Crystal, of course you can get one. You don't have to ask."

It never occurred to us that anyone else would want one. We didn't even think about it. So it became something where people just, if they felt part of it, they became part of it. Which is beautiful.

**Sounds like a great connection with everyone who lived at the house. Was this a similar feeling that you got in other punkhouses or was this unique to 309?**

Cometbus: It's always the ideal that you have a group of fiercely individual people, but you form a sort of family. Usually it doesn't last, but with 309 there's different generations, there's different waves of it, and there's people who are part of it even though they didn't live there. They're just part of it, and it wasn't about necessarily having a room there.

I would say that because it lasted, that changes the way people feel about it. Sure, there were other great houses that had a good family spirit and people doing cool stuff. My girlfriend lived in a punkhouse for twenty years that's still going in Oakland, and it has a good feeling. I think 309 is particular because it was open as a semi-public thing. It was open as the Spare Change Cafe, and they did house shows. I don't think it was totally unique, but because of the food, because of the house itself—it's an old wooden house that feels good, and it's huge—and mostly because of the fact that it lasted, all made it a little bit different than other places I lived.

One other difference is that a lot of the places I lived were all younger people, and I was younger too. 309 was always younger and older people both, and it wasn't just a generational rite of passage. It wasn't just one group of people going through one time in their life the way it would be at a college dorm.

**Did your experiences in Pensacola play a large part in the content of your zines at that time?**

Cometbus: No, the content had almost nothing to do with Pensacola. But my work is a little solitary. It's solitary work and something more people I knew did when we were younger. So to suddenly have a group of people who were ready to ride with me to the copy shop at 3:00 in the morning made a big difference. It might not be reflected in the content, but it made it possible to keep doing the magazine because I felt buoyed by the sense of camaraderie.

And it wasn't just with fanzines, but also a lot of the politics and history I was interested in. I had this "world leader wall" with portraits of all the leaders of the 182 generally recognized countries of the world, give or take ten. Someone would come hammering on my door, and it'd be Ickibod [Donald Yeo] and Sparky. "There's been a coup in São Tomé!"

I'd get out the red paint and we would cross out that leader and get a portrait of the new one and paste it up. It was really fun because everyone was paying more attention to the news and paying more attention to history because of the Subterranean Calendars.

And a lot of the things that began in that little incubator kept growing. Scotty went on to become a professor. He could have done it anyway, but it helps if you have this little community interested in the same stuff to egg you on. I think he began his journalistic career when Ickibod wrote an angry letter to the weekly paper saying that the paper was a piece of shit. They responded and said, "You're welcome to contribute to it." So Scotty began writing articles, which he does now every few weeks.

I started working at the bookstore for free and now I'm a co-owner of three bookstores here in New York, which never would have happened had I not learned the trade from Scotty and from Subterranean, which was a wonderful place to start.

**Would you say that the zine *The Spirit of St. Louis* is specifically about your Pensacola experiences?**

Cometbus: A-ha. I wondered if you would ask. No, I wouldn't say that.

I think Scotty would say that [laughs]. You can put "insert laughter." No, I don't. I wouldn't say that.

**You knew the question would come up, I'm sure.**

Cometbus: Right. Well, there *is* a magazine about Pensacola that I'd like to talk about. I don't know if Scotty mentioned the *Fish Cheer* in his interview, but in the "sixties"—sixties in quotes, because I think it may have more been '70, '71, '72—Pensacola had an underground paper called the *Gulf Coast Fish Cheer,* and their office was just three blocks from 309, in between 309 and Krispy Kreme. We would go there and sit on the porch of the old *Fish Cheer* house because we recognized them as our forbearers, but we couldn't find the people involved, and that bugged us. We were a little different than they were, but we lived in a group house, we published underground newspapers, and we were three blocks away. It just happened that there was twenty-five years in between.

We sat on the *Fish Cheer* porch almost every night, paying tribute and trying to understand our place in the larger history. We also wrote about stuff like the local streetcar strike at the turn of the century. We were trying to combat the idea that the history of Pensacola was only one of killing abortion providers, and a history of oppression. We were looking to create connections, not just between things happening in Pensacola at that time, but also in the larger sweep of history. That may sound too self-aggrandizing, but we didn't feel like we were unique, and like we had created what we had out of nothing. We really wanted to be part of this whole continuum.

The fact that what we made was able to continue on is an amazing blessing. The *Fish Cheer* house twenty-five years later was a quilt shop with no trace of its old history, but 309 twenty-five years later is still thriving, so I think we succeeded a little bit better in establishing that the underground is part of Pensacola's history. The general culture may be conservative, and that's fine, but there's other opinions and stuff happening that shouldn't be dismissed or ignored.

Scotty eventually did find the *Fish Cheer* people, though. When we'd go to the post office there was one woman who was extremely nice— the only person at the post office who didn't hate us. Turned out she was Magic Pat, the editor of the *Fish Cheer.* She'd been right in front of us all along.

One other thing I want to mention is Scotty's house arrest. We were doing so many things and he was sort of overwhelmed. He decided to put himself under house arrest so he could get some reading done and couldn't receive visitors. He actually built a jail cell in his room at 309 and got a striped outfit. He was under house arrest for several days, but eventually we found that he had put a mannequin in his bed and escaped. I think he was probably at Whataburger. It was convincing. We really didn't know that he'd made a break for it.

**And to Whataburger, no less! Do you think the 309 Museum project embodies the same excitement and energy that the house had in the early 2000s with all the projects that were in play then?**

Cometbus: Oh, I don't think anything needs to embody the same energy or the same excitement from some other time. Besides, the energy and excitement happening then was a little schizophrenic. I'm proud of it, and it's fun to talk about, but I don't know that it's what I would want right now. I mean, I still have a lot going on, but that suits my personality—it's not important that everything has that same manic energy. The only thing important is that there's a community space that would be nothing otherwise, and probably worse than nothing.

Looking back, I think we were a little desperate. We wanted desperately to keep the culture going. We wanted so badly to keep our scene alive and our group and house intact, but there was no sense that it would work. I don't think anyone could have imagined that we would own the house and that it would be a museum and an ongoing project. So it's a different energy, but in a sense it's more exciting.

**Do you have any hopes for the 309 Museum and what it can offer Pensacola?**

Cometbus: I'm not worried about what it can offer Pensacola. I think that groups need—well, most of us are atheists, but it doesn't hurt to have a church. It doesn't hurt to have somewhere where when you die they can have a service. When you get hurt, they can have a benefit. When you get married, they can have the wedding. It's incredibly important to have a grange hall, to have a union hall, to have a hall for your group. Just having a space that's yours. I think what people can offer their communities and their cities is often just to live a fulfilling life and make it look good. Of course we want to make Pensacola more exciting and cooler. But we're a vibrant subculture that has never been allowed to even consider the possibility of being included in Pensacola's official history. You know, until they gave us a closet at the—what's the museum that has the Punksacola exhibit?

**T. T. Wentworth.[3]**

Cometbus: Sure, and it's great to have this exhibit. But punk is one of the few cultures that have persisted without any outside funding, without any outside recognition except hostility from the press and from the authorities—persisted for decades, and played a significant role in the city's culture. It doesn't hurt to finally be included. I think that's where you start. You start with like, look, we are part of the art scene, we are part of the cultural scene. Whether we choose to interact with the city or if we focus on our own needs, that's the choice of the people on the 309 board and the people that go to the 309 Museum and support the museum.

**Were there any questions I may have missed that you would have asked if you were conducting this interview?**

Cometbus: Definitely [laughs].

**Well, what would be one of them?**

Cometbus: Well, you're interviewing me. When I interview you, it'll be different questions. I will say, in terms of leaving, I left because the war came. We did our best. If every city the size of Pensacola had worked as hard and shown up on the street as much as the anti-war people in Pensacola did, I think we might have stopped the war. We really put up a valiant effort on every front. But after a year or so, it became depressing—and nineteen years down the line, it's still depressing, but people have just internalized it.

You have the city that you love and you have a country that, I'm not sure we love it, but we have some warm feelings about it. Then to just see it go down the tubes. Because of the war, a lot of the connections we made dried up. Even where it didn't completely divide the population, it made things tenser. The Gulf Pride shop closed, a lot of things closed. The social interactions became tense, became closed, and the joy was sucked out of the city.

To some degree that happened to the whole country, but in Pensacola it was a double blow. First the war, and then the storm came

---

3  Following revelations that T. T. Wentworth Jr. was the Exalted Cyclops of the Pensacola KKK, the museum announced plans to change its name.

and tore everyone's roofs off. Everyone was always struggling a little but getting along. It just became a little too dear. Money was tight, social interactions were tight. But I also didn't have a bigger view of it. The people that stayed, I think they understood what was going on all along, and either they had a little less hope or they didn't expect change so quickly. But for me, I was surprised. Because what was good in Pensacola was just the best. Never, never been that good, but suddenly it felt too small. So that's why I left.

# Gloria Diaz

## "To say it was a shitty old house is an understatement"

**To start, can you tell me about yourself some? Where were you born?**

Diaz: I was born in Columbus, Georgia. My father was in the military, but we didn't live in too many places—just in Panama, on the Panama Canal, when I was very young, and then we moved back to Georgia. I lived in Fort Benning until I was thirteen. What else do you want to know?

**Tell me about your parents.**

Diaz: My parents were both born in Puerto Rico. My mom moved to the United States when she was two or three, and my father came when he was seventeen by joining the Army. My mom was also an Army brat. So I grew up on a military base until my father retired from the military and we moved to Florida.

We moved to Orlando, and I mostly lived in Orlando until I moved to Atlanta. I lived in a punkhouse in Atlanta called Squaresville, and we had a lot of shows in our house—it was a show house. I lived in that house for two years, then made a random decision to move to Pensacola. I had a boyfriend at the time and he and I just wanted to move to a different, random small town, and Pensacola seemed pretty random at the time. It ended up not being so random [laughs].

I don't know what goes on for eighteen-year-old punk kids now, but we traveled a lot. In the punk scene and in the anarchist activist community, the way everybody knew each other was through showing up, or going to shows in other towns and going to protests in other towns. It built this web-like network. I had gone to Bloomington, Indiana, which was at the time another punk small town, and they had this month-long punk summer camp thing. It was ridiculous. A ton of kids just invaded this little town for the summer. I basically showed up at a house and was living there for a month. While I was there, I started dating someone that had also just made the decision to move to Pensacola. It wasn't just me—a bunch of other kids from different parts of Florida had just decided to move to Pensacola.

Part of the punk culture of that time was to bounce around to all these different events—protests, music fests, political conferences. So we were in Bloomington for a month, and then this conference called the Southern Girls Convention, a feminist-focused conference. I was in a van full of punk kids driving back from the Southern Girls Convention, like, "We're all going to Pensacola!" Twelve of us showed up in Pensacola [laughs]. It was a little drama because my boyfriend was still in Orlando, and I was starting to date this other kid. I called my boyfriend and was like, "I'm not coming back." That's how we stayed in Pensacola, basically.

**How did you find out about the 309 house?**

Diaz: About 309? 309 was the center of the punk scene in Pensacola. So first I showed up at—at the time it was Van Gogh's, right? The cafe was called Van Gogh's. A lot of people were working there, like Scott Satterwhite and Paula Mayberry, and Jen Knight. You know, they were slightly older than us but they were all working at this weird cafe. I remember showing up there, and even then the cafe was the spot everybody went to when you got to town. Because Pensacola is not such a big town, you could show up at the cafe and figure out what was going on that day, where people were, who was in town, who wasn't. They even had this pamphlet that was hand-drawn about the sites—like where to hang out and get free donuts, or a scenic view, or whatever. I thought that was hilarious. Then 309 was across the street. It was across the street from the cafe, and Aaron Cometbus was living right next door.

**Okay, so you—**

Diaz: I actually moved in at that time. Other houses opened up later because there were too many people to all live in 309. But I ended up moving in. I'm sure you've been in the house, yeah?

**I have not actually been inside of it yet.**

Diaz: You haven't been in the house? [Laughs]

They're still doing some renovations, I believe, and getting the museum ready to go.

Diaz: Okay.

**So I've seen it. I've seen it from the outside, but I have not seen the inside yet.**

Diaz: I don't know what renovations are happening, but it's really a miracle that the house was still standing at all. I just can't emphasize that enough. It was barely, barely a home. It's like someone just nailed a bunch of pieces of wood together. The upstairs part of the house was an attic-y kind of space because the ceiling was slanted. There was a small bedroom in the back, there was a huge bedroom in the front with a balcony, and then there was this kind of nook that became my bedroom. Basically, I put up a bedsheet and that was my room. It had a window that looked out onto the train tracks and out towards the water.

**Can you walk me through a typical day living in the house?**

Diaz: Sure. Um, typical day. Well, it was hot, right? It's Florida. To say it was a shitty old house is an understatement. It's over a hundred years old and it shouldn't have been standing longer than thirty years. You could see through the walls. It was not a comfortable space unless it was spring or fall, so you didn't spend a lot of time in the house.

The first thing was always to go to the cafe because they had air conditioning. The cafe kind of served as a surrogate living room to the house. There was always a strong link between residing in 309 and working at, or just hanging out all day at, the cafe. When I first moved to Pensacola, you would go to the cafe, you'd go to the library and check your email, you would go to the health food store and get a snack whether by paying for it or not. Maybe you would go on a bike ride and go to the water. Subterranean Books was downtown, so you would go to Subterranean for the same reasons—because it had air conditioning and was comfortable and the owner let us loiter. At some point in the day, you'd make your way back to the cafe.

Once it was cooler outside we spent a lot of time on the porch of 309, just kind of hanging out, reading or talking with people. Because everybody came by that block. If a band was driving through town or playing, that's the first place they would go, or if there were kids traveling through town. I remembered staying up pretty late, and it amazes me. Now so much time is spent being on my phone or Netflix.

We didn't have any of that. We were filling our time with Vietnamese classes or making zines, or creating art, or reading, or learning different things together, and that was just how we spent our time.

**You mentioned not having any A/C in the house. Were there any other challenges that were taxing, or maybe different from living situations you'd encountered before?**

Diaz: Well, the house was started by people who were ten years older than we were. By the time I showed up, it had already been an established punkhouse. It already had ten years' worth of garbage, basically. People would move to California and just leave all their stuff. There were all these crawl spaces, little doors, and they led into these huge spaces that people had, over the years, just shoved their belongings into. I don't know what's going on with the renovations, but there's no doubt in my mind that stuff is still there to this day. I never even looked or opened those doors—I knew they were full of a lot of clutter. Now it would drive me crazy, but at that time it was part of the charm. It was just what the house was.

But the challenges, even in that time, were things like the plumbing. There was a bathroom upstairs that had a shower and a toilet. The shower eventually, for whatever reason, became dangerous to use. There was always this fear of taking a shower that may or may not involve you falling through the floor. They actually put a zine rack inside the shower stall, with zines in it. And there was a toilet that couldn't flush very well. We obviously weren't all cleaning the bathroom all the time, so it was pretty filthy. The downstairs bathroom is what we used mostly, and the tub always seemed to kind of be sinking into the floor.

We had a pretty serious fire ant problem, which was an obsession of Scott Satterwhite—Scotty Potty is what we called him at the time. He was always trying to kill those fire ants. People would get them in their clothes, and they would infest the house. And we of course had mice, like tons of mice that we basically ignored. On occasion they would die in the crawl spaces and we would smell that for a week at a time or more.

And then the kitchen was just—now, I would have a heart attack in that kitchen. It was just a space we used but also ignored, because it was completely infested with mice. But we cooked there, you know? It was just kind of punk. It wasn't something that bothered me at the time. Looking back, I'm like, "Maybe that wasn't the healthiest."

My parents showed up one time. They surprised me. I seriously thought my mom was going to bawl her eyes out when she saw the house. That's how bad it was. It was squalor. But to us, it was home. We didn't see it as an unhealthy place to be.

**You mentioned that this sort of state of disrepair was part of the punk culture. So what does "punk" mean to you, exactly?**

Diaz: Punk is a lot of things. For that community, it was either a vocalized or not-vocalized rejection of capitalist culture, but I don't want it to seem like it was just that. Recently someone asked me, "Oh, you were rebelling?" And I wasn't rebelling. I don't think any of my friends were rebelling. We were just trying to be free and do what we wanted to do. Not like, "I don't want to grow up and I don't want to work," because a lot of the kids were hard workers. People worked hard on whatever project they had. We all had our own personal visions of what we thought the world should be like, and we really believed in our ability to create the type of world we wanted to live in. We had faith in our ability to make things happen on our own. That could be anything from home repair to healthcare, and to not be in a system where we were paying for it or there were experts. We were just having fun, and it didn't pop into our minds that that was a negative thing. We were living off of nothing, you know? It wasn't like we were intentionally trying to be as disgusting or impoverished as possible.

**How did you get into the punk scene? You mentioned the idea of being dissatisfied with the way things are. Was it just that punk was the movement of the time and you latched onto it? Was it the punk music scene that got you into the other ideals going along with the punk movement?**

Diaz: I lived in Orlando, Florida—that's where I lived from the age of thirteen up to eighteen—and I went to University of Central Florida for a year, and got involved in animal rights protests. There were kids involved who were also in the punk scene, and there was a show space not too far from my parents' house where the kids would have meetings. In the early 2000s, there was a lot of activism around the IMF [International Monetary Fund] and World Bank, and that intersected with the punk community. There was a crossover between the cultures politically and artistically. So, naturally, if you're having a meeting in a show space, you're going to want to be with your friends and go to the show that's happening that evening. I made more friends that way. For me, anyway, there was an intersection between the development of my political ideologies and punk.

**So what ended up taking you to New York?**

Diaz: Basically, when I was in Pensacola the part of DIY culture that really resonated with me was healthcare. I got very into herbal medicine. I used to teach self-exams, like vaginal self-exams to girls in my bedroom—how to check your own uterus. There was this whole scene of mainly women that were learning about herbal medicine, alternative healing practices or whatever, and it had always been an interest of mine. I went to herb school in Asheville, North Carolina, another small town with a huge punk scene. From there I went to Portland, Oregon, another punk town [laughs] to go to school to become a community health educator. I eventually got into doing research and ended up at Columbia University. So that's how I ended up in New York.

**Wow, that's quite the trek of a journey there.**

Diaz: Yeah!

**Were the punk scenes different from each other in the places you went to?**

Diaz: I was actually just talking about this today with a friend. I came from the central Florida punk scene, which was insanely more pretentious than the scene in Pensacola. We were just way more snobby and dressed fancier—I don't know what other word to use—than the punk kids in Pensacola. I remember arriving in Pensacola and feeling like it was 1984. I was like, "Am I in a time warp or something? I don't understand this town." But everybody was so hilarious and friendly that it just melted my pretentiousness. I came off my high horse, and I'm grateful for the experience because it made me much more humble as far as interacting with people from different class structures. In bigger towns at that time, the punk scene was super pretentious, at least that I was part of. It was a lot of college kids that were pseudo-intellectual and really snobby about it, and were into the hardcore punk scene.

Pensacola wasn't like that. It was a small town. They were more into a different kind of punk music and dressed more simple and were more modest, and were from a more lower-working-class background. So it was a very humbling experience for me because a lot of our scenes, and a lot of the kids in those scenes, are from college and maybe they come from a middle-class family that they're not part of, but at the end of the day, they're still middle-class kids, right? But the Pensacola punk kids, and I think a lot of punk kids from smaller towns, are from working-class families. So it was just a different dynamic.

Also because the scenes are so small, they intersect with other scenes more. It wasn't like you only hung out with punk kids. They could hang out with the random sixty-year-old dudes that go to Subterranean, or the hippie, or whatever. You couldn't be such a snob about who you hung out with. Pensacola is a small town, so you became friends with, or started to care about, anyone you saw on a regular basis, and it didn't matter if they could agree with you.

**You created some zines. What were they like? What did you focus on?**

Diaz: My main zine was called *Negrita*. It was basically a personal zine, but I also tried to focus on identity. I'm Puerto Rican. At the time, being a person of color in the punk scene was super rare. So I talked about that, and I also discussed health issues. I would share things in the zine that I learned about—a lot of women's health issues, or things around food and fasting. And just stories about traveling, my hitchhiking stories and things like that.

**What led you to want to make zines specifically?**

Diaz: It was about processing feelings I had around topics that were important to me at the time. I had been in an abusive relationship, and I used my zine to process that a lot. It was a way of communicating without having to be so vulnerable doing it face-to-face, and being able to get it to a ton of people. It gave you a chance to express yourself visually, to create these things by hand—and there was real joy in creating something with your hands, creating images with glue and paper and scissors. At that time, Kinko's was still open and we were really into stealing from Kinko's. Scamming copies was the number one punk hobby.

I just wanted to express myself, and it was an easy and less scary way to express my emotions than being in a band or being a visual artist. Which I also did—I had art shows at the cafe. But it was less vulnerable to express your emotions and not have to deal with someone's feedback immediately. It's amazing, though. I wrote those zines when I was twenty-one or twenty-two, and to this day, I get messages from people who read the zine. Even recently, a friend of mine was in Portland, Oregon, and she walked into a counselor's office and "Top ten ways to support your friend who's getting an abortion" from my zine was on her wall. That's crazy to me! You know? I was a child!

**That's really cool. So do you think making zines helped develop any of the skills that you use today in your career?**

Diaz: One hundred percent. Just being a punk kid in general did—simple things like referring to somebody by the name they want to be called, or referring to someone as the gender they're telling you they are. Being really conscious about the language you're using. Respecting how someone wants to be spoken to. Thinking about what someone's going through. Just these little things we were eager to address head-on and figure out ways for ourselves how to deal with.

We were not always successful at it because we weren't experienced enough, or mentally developed enough. Not to sound ageist, but we just lacked the experience to deal with some of these heavier issues—really severe mental health issues, or addiction issues like alcoholism, which several of my friends had at the time. Or abortion, or sexual assault, which we tried to deal with on our own and were not successful.

The punk scene wasn't kind to everybody, but we were trying to make this effort as really young kids to address hard issues. I think the way it has benefited me is to always communicate well. It's given me a sensitivity to people that I'm really grateful for. When I left the punk scene—and I didn't intentionally leave the punk scene, but you go on to try other things—I saw that not everyone has that sensitivity.

**You mentioned the connection that you have with activism. Do you see a connection between the punk scene, specifically the Pensacola punk scene, and activism?**

Diaz: The era of punks that I belong to, being politically aware was definitely encouraged and respected. There were punk kids who it wasn't their thing, and activists who didn't appreciate how rowdy punk kids were, since we tended to be the rowdier ones at protests. But there was a lot of crossover, and that wasn't any different in Pensacola. There was always some protest going on. One of our favorite things was the annual [LGBTQ] Pride in Pensacola when there's tons of gay men coming to Pensacola and it brings out the super Christians who want to protest gay bars and gay clubs. We loved going to those and harassing the Christian protesters.

**Thank you for being so honest. I'm just going to ask you a couple more questions. What are some of your fondest memories that stick out from your time either living at the punkhouse or being involved with the Pensacola punk scene?**

Diaz: Pensacola is not an easy town to live in. Obviously, a lot of us had aspirations that led us out of living there. If you were queer or a person of color, the town didn't exactly meet other needs you had. But we had such a fucking good time and took care of each other so much, and I'm just super grateful to a lot of people from that time period of my life, some who are alive now and some who are not.

There were two things I found very touching from that time. We had a weekly dinner together as a family. We definitely struggled financially, and one of the ways to deal with that was guaranteeing that everybody had an awesome dinner at least once a week. It was a potluck meal held at 309 because it was the biggest house, and it had this super long table. We used to all come together once a week and just be crying laughing, we were cracking each other up so much.

Also, Scotty Satterwhite and I used to secretly celebrate Christmas. None of the punks were religious, but we were celebrating it in a truly secular way. We just liked to watch Christmas movies and eat those Little Debbie cakes shaped like Christmas trees, and drink eggnog. That was a secret ritual we would have with each other during the holiday season. Those are some of my fondest memories.

**Is there anything else you would like to discuss further? Anything you want to put on the record?**

Diaz: I think there were a lot of people who wouldn't have survived if it wasn't for that community—individuals that were older and had severe mental health issues or addiction issues that they've had to deal with since in a better way. I think it really was a refuge. Even just for kids passing through town who read about 309 in some zine, or heard about it, it was a refuge for us also—and not just 309, but the other punkhouses that existed close by. We all looked out for each other to make sure that we were alive. You expected to see everyone every day, and so you knew who was okay and who wasn't. That was a really beautiful thing.

# Lauren Anzaldo

### "The decision still scares me to death"

**The interview is taking place in 309. To begin, tell me about your parents. Who were they and where were they born?**

Anzaldo: My mom was actually born here in Pensacola. Her dad was stationed here with the Navy when she was born, and then she grew up in New Jersey, which is where my parents met. She didn't come back to Pensacola until she came to visit me, and hadn't been here in forty years.

My dad was born in Paterson, New Jersey, and my whole family was up in that area, for the most part. My dad absolutely loved old houses, and he would have really loved this renovation project, but he passed away seven years ago so he's not able to see 309 being renovated. I think about him a lot when we are getting things done around the house because he was really a handy man and loved old construction and the stories that houses can tell.

**Can I ask what your mom did—what was her job?**

Anzaldo: Sure. My mom is still around. I come from a very working-class family, so my dad was a construction worker and did a lot of mechanic work. My mom is a housecleaner. She runs a home-cleaning business.

**Who did you grow up with?**

Anzaldo: I was raised by my dad and my grandmother. My parents divorced when I was pretty young and my dad brought my sister and myself down to Florida. So I've grown up in Florida my whole life—not here in Pensacola but in central Florida, near Gainesville. My mom has not been a big part of my life, so in my house it just was my dad and grandma and sister.

**Do you have any special memories from childhood?**

Anzaldo: Sure, yeah. My sister and I climbed trees. We played in the yard. We did a lot of pretend. Cousins would come over. We would stay up all night, play hide-and-seek, manhunt, games outside in the dark, running around. I had a pretty happy childhood—we did a lot of imagining, a lot of pretending, a lot of family. We always had family come down from New Jersey, even if it was ten people, and they would all stay in our tiny two-bedroom place with us sleeping on the floor, and staying up late talking and watching movies.

**Can you tell me about your earliest memories of 309?**

Anzaldo: Well, my earliest memory of 309 was the very first time I came to Pensacola. This was our very first stop, if I remember correctly. My friend Jackie drove, and we pulled up here. She already knew people in Pensacola, so we were visiting. She and I had this little tradition where on spring break we would travel to different places. We were passing through Pensacola—maybe on our way to New Orleans, I'm guessing.

She said, "I know some people I want to introduce you to." We pulled up in front of 309 and just came in, because that's what people did. We didn't knock on the door. The door was open, and you just walk right in, and the very first room was Scott Satterwhite's room. We went in there, and there were a couple of people standing around talking in his bedroom. He was sitting at his desk, writing or typing on the computer. Jackie walks in with me, and she's like, "This is my friend Scott," and, "This is Lauren."

"Hey, how are you?" And then there was some chatter for a minute.

"We're just passing through for a few minutes or a few days." And then she said, "I heard there was a potluck over at somebody's house, so we're going over to see them."

**Can you describe what the house looked like back then, and maybe even whose room we are in right now?**

Anzaldo: Sure. This actually was my room at one time. I lived in this room, but there were always people moving in and out, and coming and going, so you can't say this is one person's room. What you would typically notice when approaching 309 was bikes all over the front porch, leaned against the wall or on the sidewalk. People were sitting on the porch, talking. The house was super cool, just the look of it, because it has that big balcony out front and those numbers, "309," in a really old font. They're actually wooden. We tried to replicate them, but you can't even buy house numbers like that anymore, and they have probably been there for—maybe not a hundred years, but certainly a very long time.

Then you would come into the house, and the whole entry wall on the left-hand side was just covered in flyers and stuff stuck everywhere. There were flyers all over the walls going back years. The house went through many phases, and people would bring furniture and take furniture, so it was not always the same. For a long time there was a giant record player-type thing that of course didn't work, and no one knew what it was, and it would have stuff piled on it. Maybe someone brought it over at one time. There was a very long dining room table that took up the main part of the dining room, and that would be where people would have big potlucks. People were usually sitting around there talking, sharing food, or hanging out. At some point, one of the residents—I think it was Sparky—found a giant church pew, and she brought it here, so that was against the wall. That was the back row of the table where people would sit, and later that got taken out to the front porch, so we had a giant church pew and people wrote all over it.

It was always changing. People would bring art. Kind of looked like a mess, honestly. I mean, it looked a little crazy, and people would sometimes come in that would be riding by. "I used to live here. Can I come take a look around?" Even when our contractor was working here, he said several people stopped by. "So you're renovating 309, can we look around? I used to live here." Five people came by while he was working. Other people that didn't know anything about it would say, "People live here?" People may have thought it was a drug den, which it wasn't, but you would see people at all hours and all times dropping in, and usually not the same people. "Is that a boarding house? What is that place?"

**Why did you decide to live here?**

Anzaldo: I sort of resisted living here at first. For a while, I sublet a room from my friend at a different house, which was much more short-lived, up the road. Then when she came back from traveling and needed me to get out, I moved in next door to 309 with another friend that was subletting from Aaron Cometbus. Aaron was gone for a year, maybe eight months. When he was coming back, I think I moved into

309 for the first time. I moved into the upstairs loft, which is really like a closet—it's probably five feet wide and eight feet deep. I just slept there, you know. I worked. I would go to work, come back, and it was freezing. It was winter, and it was really cold. I hated it. It was terrible because 309 had no heat. If you had a space heater, it would always go out because the fuses would blow. There wasn't enough power to run everything, and space heaters take up a lot of energy.

So I was kind of miserable. I didn't like it very much. I lived here one or two months that time. Another house was opening down the road, and I ended up moving in there with Adee Roberson and Sarah Hill. I think I lived in six different houses. I really resisted living in 309 because it wasn't terribly appealing, especially if it was cold or hot. I could live in other places with fewer people and probably have a cleaner and more enjoyable experience.

Finally I moved back into 309 and lived in this room. Scott and I were already a couple at that point. We had separate rooms. He lived here the whole time, he'd never left while I was moving to all these different places. But we weren't together that whole time—we didn't get together until 2003, and I moved in here in '04. The difference was, when I first moved in the house was full of people. There were a lot of people already here or on the wait list that wanted to live here and already had their eye on a specific room. Living in a tiny loft was not terribly appealing, but living in this room was more appealing, I could manage that. So you just had to bide your time until a room was available, which is why a lot of people would crash on couches or sleep in closets. Because they wanted to get their foot in the door and be able to move into a room once one became available.

Eventually, when I found out I was pregnant with our daughter, we began to come up with a plan. Obviously we needed certain things to be able to have a baby in the house, so we ended up taking over the entire top floor. My daughter had her nursery, and then we had our bedroom, which is the bedroom that has the balcony that faces the front of the house. Our daughter was born in July 2005, and we didn't move out until we bought our own place in '07.

**What is your fondest memory from this period?**

Anzaldo: We would have these potlucks—and it may not seem like it when I describe the ragtag atmosphere and all that, but people were really serious about cooking. It was always a competition of who could make the best vegan or vegetarian dish. I remember this one potluck where everyone was trying to show everybody else up. I lived next door at the time, and I spent all my time trying to make these fake fish sticks with tofu and seaweed. I made latkes, which are deep-fried shredded potatoes. I just slaved over it trying to make a really great thing that everyone would ooh and aah about. You bring the food, and everyone is like, "Oh, man. Who made this?"

**So what does punk mean to you?**

Anzaldo: That's a really good question. We all talk about differences in how someone would define punk. For me, it's almost comical to refer to myself as a punk because it just seems a little silly in a way. What I always identified much more with was the activism and the involvement and the engagement that goes with it. Because I didn't realize this until I was older, but I knew people who started businesses, started bands, put on shows, concerts—all-day kind of things where you invited people from all over the country. I put on this youth conference when I was in college. People felt like there was nothing that could stop them. They would be like, "I'm going to put out a record." "I'm going to write a book." "I'm going to organize this big training."

And no one ever said, "You can't do that. Who do you think you are?" Nobody ever said that. They were just like, "Cool, what do we need to do?"

A lot of the projects might have been less than successful, or maybe they didn't go the way everyone thought they would, but a lot of them did. A lot of them were very successful. And you think, "Wow, I can't believe I did that when I was twenty-one, or eighteen." It gave us this sense that we could do anything. It gave us a lot of skills—of how to talk to people, how to organize things and get people excited, and how to have fun and send a message.

That is the part I identify with even more than the music, which of course is a big element of it. I mean, I like the music—I'm not saying I don't. But I have been more attracted to the doing part of it. When I was in college in a different city, it was pretty much the same idea, although Pensacola did a lot more, or at least it seems that way. There was a lot more that came out of the punk scene in Pensacola that lasted and has been meaningful.

**So is it misleading that punk is all about the music? There's another side to it?**

Anzaldo: Yeah, I would say. There are a lot of arguments you could get into. There are punks who just like the music, and they don't do anything. Not every punk you meet is writing books and putting on big events and leading protests or doing anything specific, but all the people that I was around were—or at least a lot of them—and there were enough of them that it made a big difference.

Some of it you would not identify as punk. "We're going to have this book club," or, "We're going to learn Vietnamese," "We're going to have these talks about historical figures." We were always creating ways to have fun and to keep ourselves entertained and learn something. You know, not everybody does that. There was a certain element that went along with the music and the whole genre that people who are outside of it might not recognize.

**Can you tell me about your decision to purchase the 309 house?**

Anzaldo: Yeah, well, hopefully I won't regret it terribly. The group that was doing the 309 Museum project—which I am not officially a member of—were trying to figure things out. They were trying to raise money. They were having events. They were doing all this stuff, and it just didn't quite seem like it was working. Things weren't happening quickly enough.

I don't know if anyone else is going into this story, but J.P. and Michelle MacNeil owned the house. We knew them. We were friendly with them, or at least cordial with them, more so Scott because he was a long-term resident. At one point Scott said to them, "We'd be interested in buying the house," and they had a meeting. The 309 Museum group at first were like, "Will you give us the house?" I think the MacNeils were like, "No, we are not going to give you the house." Then they had a meeting where they set a price, and they said, "We'll give you a year to raise the money."

That's the part that wasn't happening quickly. A year had gone by and they really had not raised that much money. I remember Scott and I talking one night, and I said, "What if we just buy the house? What if we just do it ourselves?"

And he was like, "Do you think we could do that?"

This part of town, too, was up-and-coming. It had pretty much been the same for a couple of decades: a fine, maybe lower middle-class neighborhood, but it wasn't growing or getting bigger. Of course, going back ten or fifteen years ago, downtown wasn't like it is now.

Nothing was open on the weekend. We would want to go get something to eat, and there was nothing open.

From the mid-2000s until now, things started growing in downtown Pensacola, and people started talking about moving downtown. But there's only so much land downtown, so where are they going to move to? That's when Old East Hill became a place to go. So at the time we were looking at buying, it was like, "We need to do this now because if we don't do it now, the prices are going to keep going up and up. And more than likely the MacNeils will sell it to someone who's just going to tear this house down to the ground and build a set of condos like they put in across the street."

So there was a sense of urgency. The neighborhood had begun to change, and people realized that they didn't want the neighborhood to change, and certainly didn't want to see this house torn down and something else built here. So we pushed and pushed and were able to raise some of the money for the down payment, and then Scott and I were able to purchase the house.

We'll still see how it goes. It's kind of amazing to think as I'm talking about it that this house could have been torn to the ground. The cost was continuing to go up, and it would have been out of the price range of just about anybody other than a developer. The decision still scares me to death, and really worries me about how it's going to go. But at this point in time, it's rewarding to see what has happened and how far we've come.

**Can you tell me about the challenges of owning the house?**

Anzaldo: Well, we've only owned it now just under one year. We're about to have one year on April 1st—that was the day we closed on the house. The main challenges thus far have been just getting the construction finished. We have a mortgage and an additional construction loan on top of the mortgage to pay for all the work that needed to be done. This contractor came and looked at everything—looked at the roof, plumbing, electrical, all that stuff that had to be redone—and gave us a timeline. It was supposed to be done in six months, but it wasn't even close. Even now today, we are sitting here on February 29th, which is almost a year after that all began, and it is not finished.

The challenge was that we had to be constantly contacting this guy and coming and checking on it. You know, he's a great guy, a really excellent general contractor. I'm glad we picked him. I'm glad. We couldn't have asked for a better person because he cares about the house, and he likes old houses, and he likes doing this. We just kept running into unexpected problems, and when you get into construction, it costs a lot of money to fix things you are not expecting. Everything is budgeted to the penny according to this loan, and we had no extra money. You cannot avoid putting in new floor joists if the floor is going to fall through, but what if you don't have the money to do it? So that's a huge challenge, it really is. It was kind of fun, kind of interesting. I learned some things, but I wouldn't want to do it over again.

**Was there anything that was easy about it?**

Anzaldo: I wish I could think of something that was easy. I mean, it was easy in that I didn't have to do the work myself. He did it. He was easy to work with, for the most part. I don't mean to say he was a pain, but I just wish it would have happened a lot faster. I'm glad we had him as the contractor because he was open to our complaints and our ideas. He didn't give us a hard time. That was probably the easier part of it. But it wasn't terribly easy, no.

**Can you tell me about your role in the 309 Museum?**

Anzaldo: The 309 Museum has a board of directors, and I'm not on the board of directors. My role is more in trying to get this house to a place where it was able to pass inspection, and is livable, usable, and safe. I have some ideas, but I think my role—to be really honest—is more as the owner representing what is going to be best for the longevity of this house.

It's kind of ironic, you know. We were punks. We were young. It was anything goes, for the most part. We thought about how what we did impacted other people, but we did not think about long-term planning. But this house, we want it to be here, which means it has to be maintained. It has to be paid for. Taxes have to be paid. Broken faucets have to be fixed, so it doesn't leak and rot.

We didn't think about that kind of thing. We didn't care. It wasn't our house, even if we lived here. Now it's our house, and you can't keep a house by thumbing your nose at everybody else and just doing whatever you want. You have to take care of it. So, that's not necessarily the role I wish I had, but that's my role.

**Where is the project today? Do you think it's almost done, or do you still have a lot more work to do?**

Anzaldo: When you're talking about the project, there are different pieces of the project. You probably know this, but maybe you don't: when we bought the house, it wasn't level. The floors were rotting. The plumbing was broken. The electrical was bad, had already been bad twenty years prior. The house was really unlivable, unsafe, and uninsurable. You couldn't insure it. You couldn't live in it. You really couldn't do anything legally or safely, so it had to be completely re-done. So in terms of that, the house is good. It may not look—it's shabby chic, you know, whatever. It's kind of meant to be that way. But it has all new electrical, all new plumbing, a new roof, new wiring, new washer and dryer, dishwasher, kitchen, bathrooms. All that kind of stuff is up to date. It has an HVAC system, air conditioning, heating. In terms of all that, I'd say it's 98.5 percent finished.

But in terms of the big 309 project, the vision is to turn this building into a space for exhibiting not only the history of the house, but of the punk scene in Pensacola and beyond. Having an archive, having a re-cording studio, having an artist-in-residence space. All of those things are at different phases of completion, but that's probably twenty to forty percent finished. A lot of the artifacts and the actual exhibits and installations of what's going to be hung on the walls are already in existence at the Punksacola exhibit that opened up at the Wentworth almost two years ago. So a lot of that has already been created, but it's not been put in. We had to get the house in a workable state before we could bring anything in. We got to the top of this hard hill that we had to climb, and now we can start coasting and having events and letting people see the house and more of the vision of what the project actu-ally is.

**Where do you see the 309 Museum in five or ten years?**

Anzaldo: You know, ten years is awfully far. I had no idea ten years ago that I would be sitting here doing this right now, so it's hard to predict ten years from now. But I'll say that in five years, I think the house will be thriving. It will be full of life, and people will be coming in and out. We'll have artists, with an emphasis on diverse artists—you know, transgender individuals, people of color, women, and just people on the fringes of different elements of art and music, and visual arts and performing arts—being able to stay here and do art in this space again. Having events, having receptions to show off their work, film screenings, things like that. It would be a place of life and art and excitement and creativity and innovation, emanating positive and good information and vibes through the community as a center of creativity and inspiration for others.

**So the end goal is to be, like, the centerpiece that things flow around?**

Anzaldo: I don't know if I would say centerpiece. That seems awfully self-centered. More like an incubator—people bring ideas here, and then they're shared here. We're open to what you have to say about punk and creativity and art and history and music, so come here and share it with us, and let us give it a platform to reach our communities, and to share it with the university and the downtown historic area— people who may not otherwise be exposed.

**So, overall, why is 309 significant to you? You've already explained a lot of it. But what's really driven you to do all this? It's amazing.**

Anzaldo: Gosh, why is it significant to me? It's significant because of memories from a time that formed and shaped who I am, but it's not who I am right now. Maybe to even get a little kick in the butt looking at all the stuff I was doing back then. Maybe I need to refocus on some of that energy and youthful hope, or that spark that was happening with friendship and with community and art and creativity.

To bring us full circle, one of the first places I stepped in Pensacola was on this ground, on this floor, and my whole formative early twenties were shaped around people living at 309, or people who had lived here. Then I had my daughter living here, and met Scott, and all the other stuff. So it's just been a huge part of my life. That's my story. Other people are going to have other reasons why it's important for them, but that is what it is for me.

# Donald Yeo

"I was probably
a nightmare roommate"

**The interview is taking place at the 309 Museum. To begin, I'd like to ask some background information. Where were you born?**

Yeo: Pensacola.

**Tell me about your parents. Were they born and raised here?**

Yeo: My mother was born in Mississippi, but she was raised in Pensacola. My stepfather grew up in an orphanage in New York City and joined the military. My mom married him later on in his life while she was still young.

**Did you get along with your parents?**

Yeo: I'm an adult child of alcoholics, so it's a mixed bag. All families are mixed bags. My grandparents helped raise me a lot.

**M-hm.**

Yeo: My mother was kind of a workaholic and my stepfather worked nights. My teenage years, we started butting heads. My stepfather had a lot of issues, and I met some punk rockers, one of whom had a borderline personality disorder and really pushed me in a bad direction. I got in trouble with the law quite a bit and then was sent to military school.

**How was your schooling? Did it affect you in any way?**

Yeo: I've always been a big reader, and that's the only reason I'm not a total moron right now. Because I was stubborn, I took pride in doing badly in school. I only started going to college in my thirties, and I did well as an adult, but at school as a child I was very willful. But as an anarchist punk we read a lot—it's part of the subculture. It's also how I coped with being in military school.

**What were your earliest memories of the 309 house?**

Yeo: It was pretty opaque from the outside. You know, people like Skott Cowgill, Rymodee, Jen Knight, Shari Rother—all the Sluggo's people—seemed mysterious and cool. I'd been a punk since I was fourteen, but they seemed like they understood what was happening and I was just a poseur trying to figure it out.

**So that's what drew you to the place?**

Yeo: I think just because it's one of the last-standing centers of infrastructure, it's getting a focus that is undeserved. There were a lot of things going on at the time, and 309 was just one of them. Yeah, I was drawn to the elders of that scene, but I don't think the house itself was the draw. The people were the mystery behind it.

**Could you tell me about the neighborhood at that time?**

Yeo: It seemed a mix of middle-class and working-class black and white people. It seems a bit whiter and more middle class these days. At that point there was some bohemians, there was some working-class people. They seemed to get along fine.

**Can you describe what the house looked like then and how it was arranged?**

Yeo: It's always had a weird artwork hodgepodge—lots of cool flyers and shitty flyers, but they were arranged in such a way that the shitty flyers still looked cool. There was always some band coming through or some traveler sleeping on the couch outside. It was very active. Again, I feel like you are focusing on this one house, and there were dozens of punkhouses. Well, dozens might be an exaggeration, but there were at least a dozen punkhouses, and they all had that character. 309 had one of the most hands-off landlords, so it accrued more layers, but all of them had lots of visitors, lots of bicycles outside, that sort of thing.

I don't think the landlord ever came inside. The flip side of that is that if anything broke, he straight-up wasn't going to fix it, no matter what. He had an aversion to fixing the house.

**Could you walk me through a typical day at the house?**

Yeo: I lived with Scotty and Lauren, and it was right after Maddy was born, so they were doing their thing: raising a child, going to work and school. You had other people who worked their shitty jobs or didn't have jobs. I'm not sure there was a routine day just because of the chaos of having a bunch of roommates living together with their own agendas that didn't always intersect.

**What was your typical routine when you lived there?**

Yeo: I ran a mail-order distro,[1] so I would be answering mail or folding zines. I had a photocopier in my room, so I might be printing things. One of the things I miss about 309 is that I was better at just hanging out and chewing the fat with people. I would work for hours on various activist things—sometimes we would organize protests, and that was a flurry of activity. But it seemed like there was more downtime, and you could spend hours on the porch just chatting or playing cards.

**What were your fondest memories during this period?**

Yeo: I started a puppet troupe while I was here, and that was cool. I liked dumpster diving. I was probably a nightmare roommate, to be honest, just with the dumpster diving alone.

**Tell me about this puppet troupe.**

Yeo: We used it as a way to talk about the police. I think we performed once at the library and once at Sluggo's, and then I moved. I formed a puppet troupe with a guy I met and became good friends with in North Carolina, and did that for a number of years touring the country. It was all political activism through puppet shows.

**Did you make any friends while you were here?**

Yeo: Yeah. Friends, enemies—you name it.

**You made enemies here?**

Yeo: That's an exaggeration, but I don't necessarily get along with all my ex-roommates. Cody was a terrible roommate. Ruby was a terrible roommate. I found them challenging. Me and Ryne Ziemba butted heads, but I think it was more my fault than his. But Cody and Ruby are just unabashedly terrible people.

**Just to let you know, this is on the public record.**

Yeo: That's fine, totally fine. Cody's dog shit on the floor constantly, and he wouldn't clean it up. It was terrible, and I hated it. Ruby threw all of Kymber's stuff out on the street. It was awful, and I think she's just a bully. Totally on the public record, I'm fine with it.

---

1   A small DIY business distributing zines, books, and records, often on a not-for-profit basis.

I just—there's a thing called legal defamation so they can get into some . . .

Yeo: [Pounding on the table] Cody did not clean up his dog's shit!

[Laughs]

Yeo: [Pounding on the table] Ruby threw Kymber's stuff out on the street! She was a bully! I stand behind these statements.

**Yes [laughs]. I guess on that note, why did you leave the house?**

Yeo: I was leaving Pensacola, is why I left the house. If I was going to stay in Pensacola I would have stayed in the house. My problem was Pensacola, not 309.

**If you could go back in time, would you have still moved into the house, and why?**

Yeo: Would I have still moved into it? Yeah. The rent was cheap. It was so cheap. I'd kill for rent that cheap right now. Not literally. It was a cool house to live in—you had space to work and you got to live downtown. You could ride your bike to work.

**Where did you work during that time?**

Yeo: I'd rather not say.

**Okay. Can you tell me about your introduction into the Pensacola punk scene?**

Yeo: Sure. I was a teenager. I had a friend who was getting into punk, we watched *The Decline of Western Civilization* and tried to emulate that. I would go to shows at the Nite Owl. Sneak out and get into trouble, that sort of thing.

**What did it feel like to be in the punk scene during that time?**

Yeo: As people we're looking for identity, purpose, and meaning, and punk or any subculture provides that, so that feels good. You're getting dopamine, you're getting friends, you're getting peers—those things feel good in your brain. I felt like a poseur, for sure, but I was really trying super hard. If there was a checklist of things you could do to be an anarchist and a punk, I was trying to check off all of them.

**Would you consider yourself punk?**

Yeo: Then, I was certainly punk. At the times I wouldn't call myself punk, I was probably even more punk. These days not so much.

**Do you miss it?**

Yeo: As hard as I tried to be a punk and an anarchist, I prefer being a professional healthcare worker because I feel even more competent and able to do things in a way that I think DIY is lacking as an ideology. There was that whole attitude, "I read a zine on it and I'm going do it." Whereas chemists and scientists spend years and years learning how to do things. We're telling people that if you read a zine on being a bicycle mechanic, that's a way forward to be special and interesting. I think that's a very childish view of things. Having worked harder than I ever have to become a nurse, and some of the things I've seen since becoming a nurse, it's a little painful how naive some of us were. The problem with DIY is that it's about art.

**M-hm.**

Yeo: We pretend like the be-all-end-all of punk is art. The people who rise in it are people who are good at various forms of art, whether it be music, writing, or whatever. If you're a great artist, sure you can survive, and you can make it in the DIY scene. Or you can work a shitty coffee job or restaurant job, and do your hobbyist art, and then punk will pretend like your hobbyist art is super important.

I think we should have been more realistic about the economic realities. Some of us aren't artists, some of us are bad at art. *I'm* bad at art. I mean, I try hard at everything I do, like my puppeteering, but I'm not gifted and talented at it. So to pretend that's the thing I should do rather than the hobby I do when I'm not at work is a reversal of priorities that doesn't make sense for working-class people.

**Yeah.**

Yeo: I'm just spitballing here.

**We covered some of the, as you put it, naivety of the movement. What would you say would be the positive aspects that come out of it?**

Yeo: I like the vandalism and destruction of things that should be vandalized and destroyed.

**Why did you become a nurse?**

Yeo: It was time for a midlife career change. I was done volunteering the majority of my time and not getting paid. I had some friends who were nurses that convinced me that I would be good at it. I think that's true—I am good at it. I'm not amazing, but I think it's easy to be compassionate with people. I like the science and I like helping people through life's journey.

**Would you say that the punkhouse helped inspire you to become a nurse?**

Yeo: Wow, you're really trying to bring everything back to this house. I mean, one of my best friends is a nurse and I was living at 309 with her. I was in the band Rhythm Revolt with her, and I helped her raise her kids for a number of years. Her name is Amy. She's one of the people that convinced me to become a nurse instead of an electrician. You win! Okay [laughs].

**I got these questions!**

Yeo: I'm kidding with you.

**No, it's all good. I heard you say you were an activist during the Iraq War.**

Yeo: The one that's still going on?

**Yeah, that one. So what did you do as an activist?**

Yeo: We tried to spread information about how it was bad, and raise awareness through protest. The common thought was that protest presence in a place where so many military people were trained would help demoralize the troops. Didn't work.

**Would you have done anything differently?**

Yeo: Yeah, I would've invested in Amazon. Invested in Netflix, for sure. I would've sold all of my Blockbuster stocks. Yeah, I would've done a couple of things differently.

**I mean, would you have done anything differently with activist stuff?**

Yeo: You're asking someone at forty if in their twenties they would want to make the same mistakes? No, I would not.

**Some specifics?**

Yeo: I don't think that we were wrong, and I don't think I was wrong to do it. I just think it was hopeless.

**Are you associated with the 309 Museum?**

Yeo: No, I'm not. Me and Scotty, we hang out and visit Steve Winfrey at the nursing home when we can get a chance. But the answer is no.

I'm a fan. I'm cautiously excited about it. I think that the Wentworth exhibit was a major accomplishment, and I'm waiting to see what happens with the house.

**Why are you cautious?**

Yeo: It seems like a lot of money and effort and resources, and I'm curious to see what that turns into. I think the T. T. Wentworth exhibit is such a win with so little resources, comparatively. I think it's a super subversive thing, having so many people see this thing and interact with it. I know they put a lot of work into setting it up, but I don't think there's been much to maintain it, whereas there's a lot of work up front that goes into 309, and all the loans, and it's still not done. That's a lot of effort. What is the impact going to be? I don't mean it to be ugly on them. I think they're very ambitious and their vision is awesome. Probably in twenty years, I'll be eating my words.

**What do you think the impact will be?**

Yeo: I have no idea at this point. I hope it's interesting and pleasant to look at from an aesthetic perspective. I hope it's successful, and accessible to normal people. I hope they structure it in such a way that they don't have drama.

**If you're not associated with the museum, can you tell me why not?**

Yeo: I have a career and a family. I chat with Scotty about it. I mean, going to visit Steve Winfrey is almost a secret extension of the 309 Museum. Steve fed us for a number of years, and he has multiple sclerosis, which is such a hard disease. I was inspired to see him because his daughter came into Open Books. Scotty was telling her about the 309 Museum, and she was like, "Y'all should visit him."

I was like, "Yeah, we should. What the fuck is wrong with us?" So we did. Me and Scotty did. We brought Steve to the Punksacola exhibit. Aaron Cometbus came to visit him with us. I think we could be doing more, but this is the extent of what I can do now. So I guess my answer is, I'm secretly involved with the Steve Winfrey Support Committee.[2]

**Why is 309 significant to you, if it is?**

Yeo: Again, there's a focus on the house that I don't have. The question is: Why is a historical museum for the punk scene in Pensacola

---

2 Steve Winfrey died in April, 2020.

significant? Is it nostalgic? Is punk dead and this is just a monument to it? Is it alive, and this is a new institution that creates things of value? I think it's interesting, but I'm not sure I would say it's significant. They've already wormed their way unapologetically into the T.T. Wentworth Museum. That was significant.

**What would you say is significant about the community that fostered and grew here?**

Yeo: Significant is so hard. The punk scene did some interesting things that we can't know the significance of because we're not omniscient narrators. It's hard to know, for example, if the hundreds of zines that were encouraging children to commit crimes had some kind of impact on Pensacola. What is the lasting impact of that? Some of them wrote their names on bathroom walls, drew penises somewhere. Cool. Someone had the experience of seeing nihilist poetry on a bathroom stall. Then all the ways that the things we did changed us because we're bolder people more willing to act—or more cautious, fearful people who had a bad experience when we crossed those lines.

I think it was largely a force of positive chaos in a world that wants negative order.

**I really like the aestheticism of that. Is there anything else you want to say?**

Yeo: I probably do, but we should stop while we're ahead.

# Valerie George

## "I teach punk philosophy"

**To begin, when and where were you born?**

George: I was born in Atmore, Alabama. Yesterday was my birthday, February 26th. In 1975.

**Tell me about your parents. Who were they?**

George: My dad was a truck driver and my mom was a home health nurse who eventually started working for the Atmore public health department. She managed it after a while and retired from that position.

**Do you have siblings?**

George: I did. I have some living siblings left. My sister Denise is still with us, and my sister Angie. My brothers Don and Jim are both passed.

**Are you currently in a relationship?**

George: I am. I've met a lovely human being who lives in Mobile.

**That's wonderful. How long have you currently been in Pensacola?**

George: Oh, goodness. I moved back here in 2006 with the intention of only staying a year, but the University of West Florida offered me a full-time position, and that's all she wrote. Been here ever since.

**So what is it that you do in Pensacola?**

George: I am a full professor of art. I teach primarily sculptural classes, but all kinds of things fit under the umbrella of sculpture: plastic arts, wood, metal, and also video performance-based work, sound and noise. Pretty much all of it.

**What is your favorite type of art to do?**

George: I think as life goes on you just try a little bit of everything, so I don't have a favorite thing. Typically I work with videos, sounds, sculpture, performance, noise. Currently, I'm working on a video installation.

**Alright, how do you explain punk culture?**

George: Oh, that's so hard. It might be easier to talk about what got me into punk twenty-five years ago. I found myself an outcast in Atmore, Alabama, being an artist and a weirdo and someone who refused to call people ugly names because of the color of their skin, and I was looking for people who also felt that way. Popular culture, at least what I was encountering, didn't talk about the things that were really happening in my life—things that had to do with sexual assault, had to do with poverty, had to do with drug addiction, had to do with growing up in the South raised by a single mom with nobody to help. And when I moved to Pensacola, I found a group of people whose experiences were the same. We also tended to like the same kind of music because that music was talking about the kind of issues we thought were important.

So that's what I saw back then that I fell in love with, and that's what I think is still happening here. It's not always perfect. I'm not saying punks are perfect, but I do think that they try to be aware. Certainly, the punks I surrounded myself with raised my awareness of the world.

**You consider yourself a punk, or a member of the punk culture, correct?**

George: Yeah, I think so. There are people that would be like, "She's not punk, she's a college professor." I get that too. But I feel like I am operating as my most authentic self, and that's the punkest thing you can do.

**Was there a punk scene in Atmore growing up?**

George: There were five of us, friends I essentially met living on my block. I remember driving to Pensacola to see shows at this all-ages venue called the Nite Owl. That's when I first met the kids that lived in 309.

**How did the two scenes compare, Pensacola and Atmore?**

George: The Pensacola scene just took the Atmore kids in. We were so small, it was just like, "Come on over." We sort of converged. A lot of the Pensacola kids would come to Atmore and hang out and have a good time and go country. We would have bonfires, tie garbage can lids to the back of trucks and sit on them while the trucks drove us around in the green expanses of football fields during the summer. A lot of us didn't have parental guidance, so we were just doing whatever we wanted to do. The Pensacola kids were in similar boats, so whenever anybody had enough gas money we would load up to see one another, and we kind of shared space at each other's houses.

**When you first came to Pensacola did you live at 309 or any of the other punkhouses?**

George: You wouldn't have called the places I lived when I was younger punkhouses. A bunch of them I lived only with other punks, but they didn't function like 309—it would be an apartment and we'd all be paying a regular amount of rent. But I lived in the Javelin Joint when I moved back here. So I've lived in lots of punk spaces but technically only one punkhouse, if that makes sense.

**Were you involved with any of the zines or activism?**

George: I didn't write zines, but I did record. I built a recording studio out of my car and drove around the country and visited people—other punkhouses, other musicians—and recorded albums with the car. I recorded it all DIY, and all of them are free on my website. That spirit of archiving music that doesn't have the popular industry behind it, and the money behind it—to me that was political in that it was free. You know, I'm not selling my labor, I'm doing it because I love to, and I love these people, and I love this life. Luckily, I can sell my labor as a teacher but I don't have to sell my labor when I'm making art, and that was really important to me. So that was my contribution.

**Is there a particular piece you helped record that sticks out in your memory?**

George: Tons, but for the purpose of this interview, I'll point out two recordings that were, I think, important to 309. One was Rymodee, who was in This Bike is a Pipe Bomb. Once he started doing solo work, he and I made a recording out in Chattanooga, out in the mountains. We recorded one of his songs and I got to play alongside him and sing alongside him, and that was absolutely gorgeous. The other thing I'm glad I was able to do was the very last time This Bike is a Pipe Bomb played at Sluggo's, I recorded that. That's probably my biggest contribution to what we have for 309.

**If you were a teenager now, would you still get involved with the punk scene?**

George: Well, I couldn't say that because it has everything to do with the way I was raised, and where I was raised, and the time in which I was raised. I would like to think so, but who knows? There are a lot of amazing teenagers right now that are coming to the all-ages shows. It seems to be a pretty thoughtful group of kids that are coming up—and I don't say "kids" as a derogatory term.

## How did you get involved with the 309 Museum project?

George: Scotty asked me. He just called me one day and told me what he was trying to do here. We didn't actually know each other all that well because we sort of missed each other. When I first started coming to 309 a lot, he had already moved out—he and Lauren had gotten married and moved out. I guess we just knew each other because we teach at the same university. We would see each other and be like, "Another weird punk person that teaches at the university! They're going to find us out one day." [Laughs]

But he called me up and said, "Hey, I'm trying to save 309." I'm like, "Yeah, you should, it's an amazing place. It's got a lot of history. What do you need me to do? Here's what I'm good at: I'm good at websites, I'm good at fundraising, and I'm good at writing grants."

I'm good at all that but, you know, I'm not great at a lot of other stuff. And that's where Eliza and Sean come in, and everybody else comes in. We all have our own thing that we bring to the table.

I wanted to see it happen not just for Scotty but for the community. I feel like we need it, and if we can get this place off the ground to be everything we dreamed it might be, it would be a really great thing for Pensacola.

## What role or title do you fulfill in the project?

George: Well, as a 501c3 we have to choose president and secretary and vice-president and all that junk. We just randomly did that, but it made sense that Scotty be president, and we named Eliza vice president. I think I'm secretary, but we don't really function like that—we just do what needs to be done and we do what we're good at. Eliza's really great at booking shows and has a finger on what's going on in the Pensacola scene, so Eliza does a lot of that and handles the merch stuff. I'll probably always be someone who tries to raise money and does that background work. I don't know that I'm the face of anything, I'm more in the back, making the wheels spin.

**Where would you want to see the 309 Museum head?**

George: We saved this house for several reasons. One is to keep one of our punks living in it, and that's Barrett. We're going to put him back upstairs. He's in one of the older 309 punk bands, so his band will continue to practice upstairs and record upstairs and just hold down the space where culture gets made. Then downstairs we're hoping one of the rooms holds our archives so that the public can come and sift through the archive and research and dig around. And we love the idea of having one of the rooms, preferably the front room, be an artist-in-residence program so we can have punks come from all over the country to stay in the room for a month or so and do what they do—write their zine, make their art, make their music, do screen printing, whatever it is, and share it with the local community. We can have exhibitions in the main room, or they can play a show, or hang their prints on the wall, or give a talk or a workshop or whatever it is. So we want it to stay a living, breathing punkhouse upstairs with Barrett, and then have some fresh ideas moving through the rest of the house throughout the year.

**There was talk of putting a recording studio in. Would you make use of that recording studio?**

George: Me? I would be more interested in helping people learn how to record things. I would be more interested in the teaching aspect at this point in my life. But ask me in a year and I might change my mind.

**Have any of your art projects been supported by the 309 community?**

George: Tons of them. I recorded lots of people who were living at 309, and Eliza and I worked on some of those recordings together. I did several art projects that I would just call up, "Hey everybody, I'm filming on the racquetball courts. I've got beer, I just need you to act, or perform, or ride your bicycles." I often photographed shows and people in the bands, and they were my friends, so it made sense to make art with them. For me, art wasn't just sitting in a white cube and painting little pictures, it was being out in the world and collaborating with others. And in the punk scene that's what we do all day, all the time.

**Do you encourage punkiness with your students as a professor?**

George: Yeah, I do. I teach punk philosophy, we just don't necessarily call it that. I essentially teach collaboration. I essentially teach DIY.

There are a lot of art students that bring their objects to school and I say, "How did you figure out how to make that?"

"Oh, I watched a YouTube video."

"That's not your DIY, that's somebody else's DIY. Do it yourself— that's what it means."

But I try to teach them to support each other, that's the main thing we talk about. In fact, the last thing I said to them when I left today was, "There's this event happening on Saturday, these are your peers that are putting this event on. Go see them. Show up for them and support what they're doing because it matters."

I ask them to show up for each other. I ask them to help each other. I ask them to collaborate. I ask them to be careful about the way they spend their money when they're making art—because the way you spend your money has a lot to do with your political experience in the world, whether you realize it or not, and there are plenty of ways to make beautiful art that doesn't feed the machine or hurt the environment.

### What's this event that you're encouraging students to go to this Saturday?

George: A couple former students found a venue and they got together and they collaborated. They cleaned up the venue, they raised money together, then they asked a bunch of artists to bring in artwork, and they're bringing a musician over and having a show. That's making culture—and that's huge.

### What is one thing you want people to remember most about you?

George: I hope they'll remember me being kind. I'm not always kind, but I'd like to think I'm kind as much as I can be. And if they can't think of me being kind, at least they think of me being honest, because I have been.

# Eliza Espy

## 12

## "It never stopped being a punkhouse, and it never will"

**First of all, how long have you lived in Pensacola?**

Espy: My entire life, so thirty-three and a half years.

**And how old were you when you became involved in the punk scene here?**

Espy: Maybe thirteen or fourteen, because I was super into bands like AFI. Someone said, "Oh, AFI played here at this place called the Handlebar." That's when I was like, "Man, we have that right here in our own city." As soon as I could, I started going to shows, and I've pretty much never stopped.

**Can you describe what the scene was like back in the day? What venues were popular?**

Espy: When I was coming around, a generation was just coming to an end with places like the Nite Owl and the first couple incarnations of Sluggo's. I think the Handlebar was closed after the fire. The first place I ever saw a show was at End of the Line Cafe, which was called Van Gogh's back then.

**When was it that you found out about 309?**

Espy: I was in an organization in high school called the Young Feminist Alliance. It was a group that my friends and I started from scratch, a grassroots thing, and it was really difficult. We went through a couple of teachers trying to get someone to sponsor us because the administration at our school was so ignorant. At some point we were hanging out at End of the Line and someone was like, "Do you know these women who live over at the 309 house? They have a feminist meet-up." They invited some of us over.

**What was it like going to the women's group at 309?**

Espy: It was definitely a game changer for us. That's how we got involved organizing and going to protests and demonstrations, which happened a lot more frequently back then. There were a lot of issues on the table, like abortion rights, gay marriage, and the emerging war in Iraq.

**What were your impressions, meeting the older women?**

Espy: They were very cool, confident, and smart, so it was intimidating at first. But they were all so nice and welcoming to us. It was empowering to be in their presence, like glimpsing into the future of liberation beyond our parents' houses and public school. To see people living alternative lifestyles was a fairly new concept for me, so that expanded my mind to life's possibilities.

**Did their way of meeting and talking differ from your group?**

Espy: Well, they had a lot more knowledge and life experience than us, as well as the freedom of adulthood and their own living and meeting spaces, with the cafe and 309. We were in an uphill battle with the school administration, so we weren't technically allowed to discuss certain things, abortion in particular. That didn't really hold us back because there was little oversight and our sponsor was cool, but we wanted to take a field trip to Washington, DC, to protest Republican crackdowns on abortion laws, and our school shut us down pretty quick. That was something we saw all the 309 and End of the Line folks doing: traveling to be involved in movements in other places. Solidarity. They also had access to more radical sources of information, and introduced us to the world of zines and shops like Subterranean Books.

**Did you live at 309 at some later point?**

Espy: I did. I lived there for almost three years.

**And how did moving into the house come about?**

Espy: I was going through some life transitions. I had just dropped out of college. My best friend was going through some really hard stuff, and had tried to kill herself. I needed to get out of where I was living because it was becoming toxic really fast with her and her partner and me. I had just lost my job. I was like, "I don't know what to do!"

Some kids had just moved out of the loft at 309, and it cost eighty dollars a month. I knew I could swing that, so I moved into the loft. I didn't have a door or anything, it was just empty space between two bedrooms [laughs].

**What was it that caused you to move out eventually?**

Espy: I had gone through so many cycles with the house. I'd been through three major configurations of roommates, and I just got really tired of all of it. I felt like I was paying all the bills and fronting all the rent every month, and one day I couldn't do it anymore. I was in the shower and my eyes focused in a way I had never let them focus in there before. I was looking around, and I mean, I was the person who cleaned the tub and stuff like that, but I just knew I wasn't getting clean in there. I was cleaning the toilet soon after that and I just knew: this will be the last time I clean this toilet. The next month I was out of there.

**What was it like living in the house and having so many people coming and going over the years?**

Espy: The first wave of people, when I first started living there, were trainhoppers. When I moved into the loft both of the people that lived upstairs were on train trips, and one of the people that lived downstairs, so sometimes I had the house entirely to myself. That was pretty cool. But eventually everyone was home, and then partners they had met on the road came home, and at one point we had eleven people living in the house. Which was pretty dope, but, like, I'm a hermit and I like to keep to myself, and at the time I was traumatized so I wasn't always down to hang out.

Also, that was right after Hurricane Katrina so everybody and their mother was riding a train to New Orleans to try and score dope. Because heroin was super cheap, it was making a comeback. We lived right across the street from the cafe, which at the time was known as a place where traveling kids could come and hang out for hours and hours. It hadn't changed quite yet, you could still hang out there. Also, we had Hobo Beach right down the train tracks, which was not very well known except to visiting homeless people. You have to cross the trestle to get to it, over Graffiti Bridge.

What I'm getting at is that we lived in this place that was so available. You could just hop right off the tracks and be at the house. So many people were coming through and partying, and there was a squat between our house and End of the Line. It's a house now, with flowers on the porch and shit—but then it was just the boarded-up Gladys'

Country Kitchen.[1] It had been a restaurant, and people would squat in it and just shoot up in there for days. They're defecating in the house, and people had staph because they had come back from New Orleans where it was rampant. Everyone was in there using all the time, and it was hard to see that.

But that was the first wave. Eventually that cycle ended. A lot of people died, which is awful. The people in the house that were riding trains just moved on and went somewhere else. A different, younger crowd came in that was more introverted, and more about making art and music. That's when a lot more band practice started happening at the house, which was cool. You know, it was a simple life: drinking coffee, drinking beer.

**How long was it after you moved out of 309 that it stopped being a punkhouse and just ended up empty?**

Espy: It has never stopped being a punkhouse.

**It has never stopped being a punkhouse?**

Espy: No, it has never stopped being a punkhouse and it never will. It's innate to that place. It is not any one person—it's not anybody who's ever lived there. That house, I think, was built from the start to be a place where people could go who needed to rest or a place to do their work. It has a bigger life of its own.

After I moved out it did not collapse, by any means. People kept it going, and more people came into town and lived there. It cycled back on itself. This local painter who was living with mental illness moved in for a while. And Barrett Williamson, who I'm sure Professor Satterwhite has told you to interview, lived in there that entire time. He moved in during the beginning-ish, middle-ish part of my time there, and never left. Until they had to basically kick him out to do the renovations. He kept it going, you know? He stepped it up.

**The main thing I'm getting at is how the punk scene is different now from when you first got involved. How the scene in Pensacola has changed over the years.**

Espy: In some ways it really hasn't, because our punk scene has always been intersectional with so many other social and political movements.

---

1   A short-lived soul food restaurant located in between 309 and End of the Line. The owner, Robert Forney Jr., worked nights at the neighborhood Krispy Kreme.

Its values that resonated with me are humanitarian, fundamentally. I've always seen diversity in the scene, and it's always been a fun place where there were a lot of brave people being themselves. Especially back in the day, you could just come as you were—like smelly, armpit hair hanging out of the shirt you've been wearing for three days. It was a very accepting, loving place, and it still is. There were always visible queers and people of color singing about liberation.

**Where do you see the punk scene in Pensacola going in the future?**

Espy: Wherever we fucking take it! Where we going, Mars? What if I just pass the remote control on to you? I think it's important to respond to the needs of the time. You can have a plan, but life comes at you hard and fast, and nature takes its course. It's important to watch the signs and figure out how to help people, which is part of punk. Trying to figure out who needs help and how to get aid to people, and resources. The connectedness is the main thing that I would like to see grow about it—people learning how to take better care of themselves and each other. But definitely a big part of that is preserving space where bands can practice or potentially record, and people can take workshops or hear seminars. Just having space for people to go who don't feel like they fit in other places.

**To elaborate on that, what do you want the 309 house to mean for the punk community?**

Espy: In the system we're living in, there's people showing the have-nots that they can't have things. Everything that holds us back, like, "I don't have money for an instrument," "I don't know how to record," "I feel really cut off," "I can't dress how I want to dress," "I can't fully express," "I can't tell my parents who I love." Whatever it is, I want people to understand that there's people who get that and are working towards a better world for everybody, especially the most vulnerable in our society. I just want it to be a lighthouse in that way—a monument to culture that extends beyond this really oppressive system that we all have to live in.

**Do you think 309 has always existed as a lighthouse for the people who find it?**

Espy: Well, I can't really say. I'm sure you know more about this from research than I do, but it was a railroad flophouse before it was a punkhouse. I'm sure after working those long shifts it'd be pretty nice to crawl into bed for a little while.

**To wrap up, I'd like to know what punk has meant to you specifically, and your experience in life.**

Espy: It has helped me to throw down my chains [laughs]. It has taken me effortlessly traveling across the country—and maybe someday the world. And it has shown me this way of living that is so much preferable to the rat race that I see. I was looking for another way of life, and it has helped me find my own path in that direction.

# Barrett Williamson

## 13

"Everything passes in time"

**I'm here with Mr. Barrett Williamson of the band Rezolve. We're sitting down at the 309 house in the Old East Hill section of Pensacola, Florida. We're here to discuss the history of the house and the people who lived here since its inception as a punkhouse. So, Barrett, do you have any siblings?**

Williamson: I have a sister. She's a little over six years older than me. In terms of blood siblings, that's it.

**Were your parents around as a kid?**

Williamson: Yeah, I had a nuclear family. My dad joined the Navy kind of late in life, but my mom and dad got married in college in the seventies and they're still married. Pretty stable family.

**Did you move around?**

Williamson: Yeah, we moved all around. You know, military family. My earliest memories, we lived in Iceland. There used to be a base during the Reagan era, it's shut down now. I lived in North Carolina for a minute, and then California. I lived in Maryland for a while. At some point my dad shifted from being on ships as a navigator to being retrained for intelligence stuff. He got his masters and worked for the NSA for a number of years.

I was thirteen-to-fifteen when I first lived here. Then we moved to Maine, and I was in a kind of intense car accident where I was in the hospital for the better part of a year. Then we moved back here the last couple years of high school. And I've moved back and forth a couple times.

**I was going to say, you've been around. You've been to all kinds of schools, probably public schools. Did you ever get in any trouble in school?**

Williamson: I got suspended and expelled in middle school for getting in fights. The process of moving around, being displaced a lot, I probably got more and more antisocial as a result of that. You know, not really bad—well, maybe it would have happened anyway, I don't know. But other than that, I didn't really get into any trouble. I did well in school until the very end, by which point my decline didn't matter too much.

**When did you first discover punk?**

Williamson: Probably that period when we first moved here. I grew up being part of that era, and maybe it's my personality, but where you get into something and you're all-consumed, and trying to find that thing you're going to be into. My first year of high school in Pensacola, there were a couple of punk rock kids. My concerns leading up to that were like Philip K. Dick, Harlan Ellison, and, um, have you ever seen *The Prisoner*? That was my favorite.

***The Prisoner*? No, I don't think I have.**

Williamson: It's this old sixties TV show. It's sort of the first existential, deconstructionist TV show. Ostensibly it's a secret agent show, where this guy—who's like a James Bond type of character—has retired from being a secret agent and then wakes up on a strange island that's run by a weird hierarchical structure where everybody has numbers instead of names. They promise to let him leave if he says why he resigned, but he refuses to give up that information because it's a loss of personal freedom.

**Yeah.**

Williamson: And then it gets more and more elaborate to the point where you're questioning if the whole thing is a dream, or if the whole show is a kind of deconstructionist thing on the nature of reality. I was drawn to those sort of things, and it's getting to be a weird conversation already, but I guess I was looking for some kind of personal philosophy to hold on to, and the kids that had the Clash and Sex Pistols T-shirts seemed to have something they were holding onto. It was something weird, and it looked cool. A lot of art I like is essentially hyper-stylized young, masculine kind of crap, where everything looks really cool but there is some existential theme going on behind it.

**You said you're attracted to visual styles. Was it the visual of these kids who were punk that made you think they had a message and ideals?**

Williamson: At least they had the veneer of that. I don't know how much actual message was there other than very vague sentiments, but that's not necessarily a bad thing. Also there was the sense of a tribal community, which is important at that age, I guess. They seemed to be a tribe that was a clique to the side, but was still a different option. Especially when you're that age, young men—it may be a little bit different now, but I don't imagine it's that different—young guys can be morally questionable, even if they're harmless. I'm not trying to say I'm above anyone, but like a bro-jock mentality of, "I'm young and dumb and feeling the push to assert my aggression over others."

**Oh yeah.**

Williamson: So you had that, or you had the non-socially functioning academic path. I didn't see myself in either of those. This was something to the side. It seemed to have an ethos behind it even if it was very vague.

**Did your parents have any thoughts about you when you found this style?**

Williamson: I don't think they really understood it. I remember the first time, I was maybe sixteen, when it's like, "We're going to get mohawks!" Me and my best friends got clippers and my parents freaked. I remember my dad sitting me down. It was like he thought I had just been led astray and he needed to correct me. He said, "Mohawks are something we got as little kids in the fifties, when we were playing cowboys and Indians." It's like he thought I had brain damage.

Also my dad, interestingly enough, is an Ayn Rand follower, so maybe that played into his thoughts. I thought that he would find similarities when I was interested in traditional anarchist writing or philosophy. I was seeing similarities, so I thought he would be sympathetic, but it was no, not really. They didn't get it, but later on they came to be more understanding, probably just from years of being inundated by it one way or another. They came to figure out a little bit more of what it was about, or what it was about for me, and they're sweet people. I don't hold any grudges about it. It was fun, normal, kids-versus-parents stuff.

**Is that when you heard about 309, or was that later when you came back?**

Williamson: Probably when I came back. I'd started playing bass midway through the first year of high school, and I jammed with the guys that would end up being in my first band. We were starting to get things going, and then I moved to Maine for that year. I immediately got in a car wreck and was in the hospital for nine months. Then we moved back at the end of that. When I moved back is when we slowly—as I was getting more functional off of crutches—started playing together again.

The whole year I was in Maine I got a lot better at guitar just because I had a lot of time. We lived in the middle of nowhere, literally at the top of a mountain. It was a base that was being decommissioned, like the northernmost point in the U.S. They used to have satellite dishes that would intercept Russian radio signals, but it had all become disused at the end of the nineties, so my dad was in operational charge of this base as they were decommissioning it. I had to be bussed two hours away to go to a really tiny high school.

I had a couple of friends out there that I played with rarely, but it was very hard to do anything. I would drive two hours away to go to a strip mall CD store and buy whatever they had. I spent a lot of time in front of the record player, CD player, with the guitar just trying to hack it out. That got me maybe a step above the other people I was playing with by having a lot of time to mess around. Anyway, my first band was the Hazards. We used to play at Van Gogh's, which then became End of the Line.

**Mmm, okay.**

Williamson: Which was very different back then. It wasn't really a restaurant to my memory. You could get one food item maybe, but they had coffee and put on shows, and sometimes the shows would spill out from over there to here. That was my first 309 encounter. Ickibod—or Donald, but everyone called him Ickibod back then—he lived here, I believe. He used to hand out anarchist literature from the Crimethinc collective,[1] which I think was largely—my impression—a bunch of

---

1 A Chapel Hill–based group that combined adventurist lifestyle anarchism with cryptic Situationist theory.

well-educated upper-middle-class kids that got into anarchist philoso-phy.

I don't mean that as a dis; I was really into that at one point. But I've sort of grown—wary may not be the right word, but disillusioned with organized political movements of any form. That's not really relevant to anything, but I sounded like I was talking shit on Crimethinc, which I'm not trying to do. They put out some cool stuff. I don't know, not my bag maybe at the end of the day. Anyway, the first Hazards shows would be largely over there and the first time I came to the house was that period.

**Did you ever play at 309?**

Williamson: That came later. My first experience, other than wander-ing over here to look at Crimethinc propaganda that Ickibod had set up on a table outside, was when I had a girlfriend that lived here in 2006. At that point, unfortunately, I was an opioid addict, so my life was just floating around. That lasted the better part of my twenties. I went to UWF for a couple of years, and the slide into drug addiction hit mid-way into that. I won't go off on tangents about all of that, but my first experiences were in this room, staying with Kelsey, my old girlfriend. When I lived here for nine years, this was my room as well. There was a loft bed right there. I would be up there shooting dope and watching TV on the little TV right there. So this is a kind of weird experience for me on account of I've had a lot of experiences in this room.

**Were you apprehensive when you first got here?**

Williamson: I was worried about people catching on to me shooting dope, then trying to give me problems. That's where my head was at. Someone had a job as a phone sex operator, and they had a landline at the front of the house when you walked in. I was coming in to try and use the phone. My cell phone was dead and I needed to get up with my dope boy so I could make the hand-off on drugs and money. So I came here to use the phone and she was on a call on the sex-line. God bless her, man. I'm sure she had me pegged. She came out in her nightie with her headset on. "Okay, I'm going to click off, but I got ninety seconds before I've got to take the guy's call back because he's anxious. Make the fucking phone call!"

Anyway, that's a memory from old 309. For the sake of the timeline, 2010 is when I moved in here. That's when I stopped doing drugs, and I started working at Sluggo's around that time. I had gotten into writing my own stuff by myself, just doing home recordings, sort of sad bastard music. But I got into playing in two bands regularly when I moved in here.

**Being at 309 and being with the people in the community, did it help or did it hinder any habits you had? Did they help you get over it, or was it through your own will?**

Williamson: The drug shit? I don't know. One of my old street punk buddies showed me how to shoot up, so you know, not to put it on him—or maybe put it on him—but I don't want to give him the blame. I would say overall, when I was deep into the drug world, my punk rock friends were mainly separate. Occasionally they would overlap. But it wasn't, at least in my experience, and in Pensacola, the romance of Johnny Thunders or Dee Dee Ramone or Nick Cave. The punk rock junkie fantasy. It wasn't that. When you're in the junkie world, that is your ethos and it has its own rules for living. The punk rock world is sort of separate. There's definitely a doorway from one to the other, but they are separate.

I would say that playing music is hard no matter what, even if you have money. It's very hard to put your focus and attention on any kind of art and not have it suffer when you have to go through the mechanics of maintaining a drug habit. Outside of anything it does to you mentally or spiritually or emotionally, it's just a distraction. So yeah, I would say having punk to embrace was a good thing. It was a good thing having that community and that support. The second I stopped shooting up I got everything I needed to get by. Suddenly everything just sort of worked out.

**What was the neighborhood like when you first got here?**

Williamson: Not that different than it is now. I mean, you see the encroachment of what people would call gentrification. That's definitely going on, but you can still see what was here, for the most part. Maybe that will change over time, but it's not that different yet. My perception is that Pensacola might even be a little bit better. With the drug trade and stuff, maybe because I was involved in it, I see things like that visually from the outside. I feel like it was a little bit worse back then, but that's probably just my perception. Who knows? It's probably about the same.

**When you moved in, what was the house like physically?**

Williamson: Stuffed with everybody's crap, you know? When Scotty and Lauren were living upstairs, they had things a little more arranged. There was a reading area and a bookshelf and zine racks and stuff, more of a communal space. As the years followed after they left, that sort of sustained but it got messier. More kids moved in, probably too many kids moved in. They had a chicken coop back there. Too many traveling kids for the house to sustain without damage over time. But it was nice. It was a busy bustle all of the time. Lot of people running in and out. Lot of kids that had, you know, parents' houses to go to. Just different than my situation. But whatever. That's cool.

**Just for posterity, when you say kid, what age range are we talking about?**

Williamson: That's a good question. Anywhere from eighteen to thirty, probably. Not children. I still say "kids" talking about people my age in the scene.

**Were there any major factors that convinced you that you needed to move into 309? Other than community.**

Williamson: It was just a de facto thing. It was never a plan. Over time as I ended up here on my own, I felt more and more a part of it, and as the house continued to degrade, I had the feeling that the decline of the house was declining with the physical decay of my body. But that's just the way I think. It's weird, you know, I've spent a lot of fucking time in this place. It's a good chunk of my life. But it's a good house. It's obviously, on a practical level, old construction.

**Beautiful, really.**

Williamson: Whether it's true or not, I choose to think there's some kind of higher hand brushing mayhem away from it.

**Can you remember the people that lived here when you moved in? How many there were, anything like that?**

Williamson: Eliza Espy lived here. My buddy Savannah, she works at the hair salon around the corner, she used to work with me at Sluggo's. Man, a couple of people whose faces I can place but can't remember their names. A girl that came from Portland, blue hair. Kid that was sleeping on the couch and had the chickens back there that was kind of crushed on Savannah and got her dog's name tattooed on his foot.

**Mmm.**

Williamson: Also Savannah's boyfriend—he gave me this stick-and-poke tattoo. Kelsey lived here, my old girlfriend and Savannah's best friend at the time. Corey Vinegar, obviously his last name is a punk name or a made-up name. He lived upstairs. He actually was a little kid who came to Hazards shows when he was twelve or thirteen, and had really bad liberty spikes that he would glue. He lived here with his girlfriend, Christina Lagos, who still lives in town. She's the cousin of my girlfriend—or that *was* my girlfriend for many years—Lyrik Lagos, who was living with me here at the end. Crystal Tremer lived in the front room for many years. She's from here, she's an old punk rocker. I think she's living in Oakland. I could name other people that frequented the house, but those are the people that lived here significantly that come to mind.

**Were there any problems with people that lived here? Any altercations, drama?**

Williamson: Sure, but nothing so bad that I would want to defame anybody. The endless train of trainhopping kids wanting to stay here kind of got problematic. Some people are really nice and just having their adventure, living out there and having a good time and wouldn't harm anybody. Other people—and I'm not looking down on them either—other people have drug habits or are just kind of scummy. Your basic guy-in-the-woods, caveman-level problems of life, especially if you have a completely open door policy, and that's sort of what I inherited. I got burned on that, and probably overreacted too much. I probably got overly bitter and entitled—you know, the grim face in the tower. I had a couple of people who crashed on the couch that it took me a month to get rid of or more, who were sort of friends but also living rent-free and mooching off me for a long time. You get involved with their problems and feel bad for them. You can play all this stuff out in your mind. Anyway, nothing I look back on with any great bitterness. Sure, crazy shit did happen, but nothing that nobody's walking away from.

**For those that did live here full-time, how did the house operate? Were there chores? How did you pitch in?**

Williamson: When I first moved in, there was some remnant of that. I think it worked best when there were a lot of people here. When it was just me and a couple of other people, I realized I had only been in my room or the bathroom most of the time, just bee-lining in and out. There were mountains of trash piled in the laundry room. That was a project to clean. I know at one point there was a little chore wheel, and that sort of stuff. I don't have much memories of that because during the majority of the decade I lived here that wasn't going on beyond a verbal level.

**Was that just a gradual decline in the house, people moving away, or was there an event that happened?**

Williamson: It was just a gradual thing. Especially if you think of kids who are in their early-to-mid-twenties. They live here a few years, and at some point it's cold—it's colder than it is outside. There's electrical problems. It's dirty. There's, like, a hole in the floor next to you. At some point, people have had the trip. They have other options. There's no need for them to not go do something else, or their path takes them somewhere else.

It wasn't overnight. It just went from being six people living here, and now there's five people living here. Now there's four people living here. Now there's two people living here, and you're the one paying the rent.

**Were you ever worried about the fate of the house and having to move on?**

Williamson: I knew that as the attention on it as a piece of communal history grew, and people got more interested in that, it was going to fall out of my hands. But that was inevitable anyway, and it's not like I was in a position to buy it. Everything passes in time, and this fate is certainly better than many. Scotty and Lauren are really awesome people, and it looks like they've done an awesome job. If they didn't buy it, we really did believe that the owners were going to bulldoze it and build something new, or sell it to people that would, just because of the cost. I don't know if that would've happened or not, but I know that nobody else would've saved it to the level that they have. I'm surprised that it's still as much the same as it was. It's just sort of, you know: they did it. This is nice, and it's cool to sit here talking about it.

**So, overall, was it a good or a bad experience?**

Williamson: It's just my life. I wouldn't trade what I could change for losing the things I wouldn't want to.

That may have been over my head, what you just said. Would you do it again, would you move in again?

Williamson: Yeah.

**Okay, just to finish up, what is punk to you?**

Williamson: Ah, hmm. You mean like musically, or on a metaphysical level?

**Probably on a metaphysical level.**

Williamson: I guess it's just some kind of struggle to remain truthful, and, uh, keep focus, keep quick in the moment. And to be full of passion and resolve.

**Alright Barrett, thank you for talking to us. It was actually really great.**

Williamson: Appreciate you guys, man. Enjoy.

# ACKNOWLEDGMENTS

Thanks to the students in Professor Wells's oral history class who did the fieldwork on which this book is based: Emaly Allison, Landon Cagle, Rebecca Cassady, Robin Dunn, Tommy Gilliam, Sydnee Hammond, Austin Harman, Hansen Hasenberg, Kelsea Jacobson, Mars Madden, Dillon Maddox, Alexis Matrone, Ryan Obray, Bailey Phillips, Gabriel Waters, and Nick Williamson. Special thanks to Jamin Wells for encouragement, Matthew Clavin for advice, and Laura DuPont for going the extra mile to tie up loose ends.

The authors gratefully acknowledge permission to reprint passages from "My Florida" ©℗KML, 1987, and "Board of Tourism" © Ryan Modee, 1997.

Original transcripts are held at the West Florida History Center at the University of West Florida.

AARON COMETBUS has been publishing *Cometbus* magazine since 1981. He is the editor of the oral histories *Back to the Land* and *The Dead End,* and the author of seven novels. He earned a gold record using his teeth as a percussion instrument.

SCOTT SATTERWHITE is a historian, educator, and journalist. His work has appeared in *Florida Historical Quarterly, Hurricane Review, INWeekly, and Maximum Rocknroll.* He is the author of several poetry chapbooks and edits the zine *Mylxine.* Satterwhite teaches writing and literature at the University of West Florida.